CORPORATE PERFORMANCE MANAGEMENT

How to Build a Better Organization Through Measurement-Driven Strategic Alignment

IMPROVING
HUMAN
PERFORMANCE
SERIES

Series Editor: Jack J. Phillips, Ph.D.

Accountability in Human Resource Management
Jack J. Phillips

Achieving the Perfect Fit
Nick Boulter, Murray Dalziel, Ph.D., and Jackie Hill, Editors

Bottom-Line Training
Donald J. Ford

Corporate Performance Management: How to Build a Better Organization Through Management-Driven Strategic Alignment
David Wade and Ronald Recardo

Developing Supervisors and Team Leaders
Donald L. Kirkpatrick

The Global Advantage
Michael J. Marquardt

Handbook of Training Evaluation and Measurement Methods, 3rd Edition
Jack J. Phillips

Human Performance Consulting
James S. Pepitone

Human Performance Improvement
William J. Rothwell, Carolyn K. Hohne, and Stephen B. King

The Human Resources Scorecard: Measuring the Return on Investment
Jack J. Phillips, Patricia Pulliam Phillips, and Ron D. Stone

HR to the Rescue
Edward M. Mone and Manuel London

HRD Survival Skills
Jessica Levant

HRD Trends Worldwide
Jack J. Phillips

Learning in Chaos
James Hite, Jr.

Managing Change Effectively: Approaches, Methods, and Case Examples
Donald L. Kirkpatrick

The Power of 360° Feedback
David A. Waldman and Leanne E. Atwater

Return on Investment in Training and Performance Improvement Programs
Jack J. Phillips

Technology-Based Training
Serge Ravet and Maureen Layte

CORPORATE PERFORMANCE MANAGEMENT

How to Build a Better Organization Through Measurement-Driven Strategic Alignment

DAVID WADE

AND

RONALD RECARDO

Boston   Oxford   Auckland   Johannesburg   Melbourne   New Delhi

Library of Congress Cataloging-in-Publication Data

Wade, David.
  Corporate performance management : how to build a better organization through measurement-driven strategic alignment / David Wade and Ronald Recardo.
    p. cm.
  Includes bibliographical references and index.
  ISBN 0-87719-386-X (alk. paper)
    1. Management—Evaluation. 2. Performance standards. 3. Organizational change. I. Recardo, Ronald J. II. Title.

HD31 .W237 2001
658.4'012—dc21

2001025362

British Library Cataloguing-in-Publication Data
A catalogue record for this book is available from the British Library.

The publisher offers special discounts on bulk orders of this book.
For information, please contact:
Manager of Special Sales
Butterworth–Heinemann
225 Wildwood Avenue
Woburn, MA 01801–2041
Tel: 781-904-2500
Fax: 781-904-2620

For information on all Butterworth–Heinemann publications available, contact our World Wide Web home page at: http://www.bh.com

10 9 8 7 6 5 4 3 2 1

Printed in the United States of America

In Memory of
Delmer Wade

Stoic, stubborn, still
Seeking some understanding
Found the light at last

February 20, 1922 – March 7, 2000

Contents

1

Corporate Performance Management: An Overview 1

What We Know 1. Strategic Focus 2. Corporate Initiatives 5. Balanced (Corporate) Scorecards 5. The Activity-Based Business Plan 8. Process Performance Measures 8. Developing Job Performance Measures 9. The Individual Performance Profile 10. Frequently Asked Questions About Performance Measurement 12. Summary 14.

2

The Strategic Focus: The Context for All Performance Measures 17

Why Only One of Three Strategy Focuses? 18. Key Performance Measures of Three Strategy Focuses 22. Mixed Strategies 27.

Management Questions 73. Three-Phase MIS Project
Guidelines 75. Summary 80.

6

Process Architecture 82

7

The Corporate (or Balanced) Scorecard 94

8

The Business Planning Process 114

9

10

Foreword

When surveyed, the overwhelming majority of executives are unhappy with their performance measurement system. Many organizations, when asked about their performance measures, respond that they have too many. The following example is typical of many organizations. Tom Peters asked a manager "How many performance measures do you have?" The manager responded "105 measures." Peters then asked which performance measures she had to pay attention to. As you might have guessed, she responded "None of them."

Performance measurement systems have been around for many years. One would think that by now, organizations would have figured out what makes a good performance measurement system. However, surveys indicate that executives are unhappy with their systems. Why the discontent?

There are many reasons. As just indicated, most organizations have too many performance measures. Because they have too many measures, executives and middle managers don't know where to focus their attention. When an organization simultaneously focuses on cash flow, earnings per share, net profit, and operating profit, several people can have major effects on these measures in several ways. For example, the treasurer could buy back stock to decrease the number of outstanding shares. This would increase earnings per share even if profit stayed the same. Is this the result the organization wanted? The organization could increase operating profit by automating, but the purchase of equipment would decrease cash flow in the year of purchase. Is this the result the organization wanted?

Another complaint of executives is that they are not sure they have the correct measures. For example, a major European company was known for product innovation. It had numerous performance measures for manufacturing efficiency, but it was lacking measures dealing with the number of new products, the average length of time to introduce a new product, and the success rate of new product introductions. This is not an isolated example. Having the wrong or inappropriate measures is a major problem for organizations. Executives may not know the correct measures, but they do know they don't have the right ones.

Executives also complain that the performance measures are not properly communicated throughout the organization. Let's illustrate this with an example from the car rental industry. A janitor is told to keep the floors clean in areas where customers sign their rental agreements. Being conscientious and wanting to do a good job, he carries out the commands of his supervisor. The wet floors cause customers to fall, resulting in multi-million dollar lawsuits. Management really wanted customer safety as well as clean floors. However, safety was not properly communicated.

Executives complain about a lack of alignment. For example, management states in its mission statement that it wants high-quality products and services. However, as deadlines approach, management allows delivery of sub-standard products and services. Now the workers are confused. They were told the goals were quality and timeliness, however quality seems to be ignored, and timeliness takes precedence. So the real goal is quality if you have time, but always be on time. Is this the focus the executives wanted?

More and more boards are basing executive compensation on long-term results. A performance measurement system that emphasizes short-term financial measures creates long-term problems. For example, an organization can improve short-term financial performance by cutting back on research. However, this short-term focus will not meet long-term financial goals.

What about organizations that don't spend the necessary dollars training their staff in today's rapidly changing world? In the short term they may survive. In the long run their employees will become obsolete. They will lose valuable talent, because one of the reasons employees stay is that they have an opportunity to grow and develop. Without a balanced approach to measures, the organization will degrade.

What about measures that focus on the customer? Most organizations have some type of customer satisfaction measure. However, what really drives customer satisfaction? Is it product/service quality? Is it how fast you answer the phone? Is it the quality of customer support? What does the customer really want that will at the same time meet the needs of the shareholder? An organization can provide the customer with many features and support services, but will satisfying the customer in all these ways still meet the long-term financial objectives? How do you know?

Organizations are reengineering/redesigning many processes. However, on which processes should they focus? A major computer company became a best-practices company for payroll processing. It spent millions of dollars reengineering its payroll process, but it should have spent that time reengineering its research, manufacturing, and selling functions to keep them viable. As a result of neglecting these functions, its financial weakness caused it to be acquired by another computer company. Why didn't its performance measurement system show management where to focus its reengineering efforts?

Executives are frustrated because they set targets and the targets are not achieved. They don't know why they are not achieved, but they want to know which indicators will predict if they are going to reach their goals. They want a predictive performance measurement system, rather than one that is just historical. They want a system that predicts whether they are on course, and if not, what they have to do to correct and thus achieve the desired targets.

David Wade and Ron Recardo have done a wonderful job in this book of presenting a step by step approach for measurement-driven strategic alignment.

John Antos
President
Value Creation Group, Inc.

Acknowledgments

Researching and writing a book is a time-consuming process, especially when managing a consulting company. I would like to take this time to acknowledge the following individuals who were either directly or indirectly responsible for this book. First and foremost I would like to thank my wife and best friend, Diane. She provided both emotional support and patience when I was banging away at the computer instead of spending time with her. Additionally, she provided critical feedback on the content and flow of the manuscript. I would also like to thank my parents, John and Mary Recardo, who instilled a strong value set and a never-ending dedication to excellence. Their love and sacrifice can never be repaid.

And lastly, I would like to thank the many clients of The Catalyst Consulting Group, LLC. Being a consultant is akin to being a child again. Our clients provide us the opportunity to both share our learning and learn from them. Such collective learning is the backbone of this book.

Feel free to direct questions or comments to me at **rrecardo@ catalyst-consulting.net**

Ronald J. Recardo

Thanks to Sandy, whose patience and support helped make this happen; to Tim Calk for providing excellent support and guidance, and for taking over the project in the midst of Gulf Publishing's restructuring; to Elionne Belden, Ph.D., our editor, who demanded excellence from us; to Ed Selig, who first suggested this book, oh so many years ago! To John

Antos for writing the foreword. And thanks, John, for the hours we have spent discussing performance measures, scorecards, and activity-based costing.

In addition, thanks to all the reviewers for providing their input:

- Jocelyn Caputi, director, Johnson & Johnson
- Faye Craig, professor of psychology, Marian College
- M.L. LaFond, president, Cox Cable University, director of training and development, Southeast Region
- Michael Kaufman, president, Video Monitoring Service
- Gloria McCree, CFO, corporate human resources, Aetna, Inc.
- Lou Scmukler, vice-president, quality management, Hoffmann-La Roche, Inc.

David Wade

Corporate Performance Management: An Overview

1

What We Know

Business management fads come and go on a regular basis. During the last 70 years, we have seen everything from scientific management and theory "Y," to empowerment, results-based management, and spiritualism in the workplace. There are four basic concepts at the heart of corporate performance management. Managers with the highest return on equity embrace these concepts:

1. Top managers adopt a well-defined and communicated business strategy.[1]
2. Top managers close gaps between organization, technology, and process architectures. Closely aligning each element, within each architecture, greatly enhances company performance.
3. Top managers align all the activities from top to bottom within the organization. If an activity doesn't add value, managers outsource or eliminate it.
4. Top managers adopt a specific set (more than 10, less than 30) of key performance measures covering a diverse set of performance categories (e.g., employee satisfaction, customer satisfaction, productivity, growth and innovation, financial results).[2]

Business experts, business economists, and organizational psychologists all agree that management must choose a specific business strategy for a corporation to excel. Leading American managers, from multi-industry General Electric to retailer Wal-Mart, have discovered that extraordinary financial results flow from a strategy and a detailed plan to implement it. Beyond having a strategy, the managers of these top financial performers emphasize something else: a performance measurement system that ties every aspect of the organization—from the boardroom to the factory floor—to the strategy. This is known as "alignment management."

Alignment management occurs when all activities of a company bear a direct relationship to the business strategy. The combination of choosing a business strategy and adding the discipline of alignment leads to superior financial results—greater than 15% return on equity over multiple years. Companies that have consistently met that mark over the past five years by combining strategy with alignment include: Allied Signal, Coca-Cola, General Electric, Hewlett-Packard, JP Morgan, Merck, Motorola, and Wal-Mart.

Traditional corporate-level performance measures—financial and gross productivity results—have failed most corporations. Managers have become disillusioned with these "trailing" performance measures, because they have not helped them run the business. Savvy companies have learned that performance measures, diligently used, significantly affect organizational alignment. CEOs want performance measures that offer predictive power and provide a better understanding of the real costs associated with each process. Additionally, institutional investors are becoming more concerned with the long-term health and overall performance of the companies in which they invest. According to the Conference Board, many institutional investors are insisting that their portfolio companies develop a more balanced performance measurement system. Alignment management can help achieve that balance using three distinct levels of performance measures.

Strategic Focus

Frankly, for too long companies have tried to be all things to all people. They have not embraced any particular strategic focus. The business strategy is the first and most important performance measure. Take a look at General Electric. By the end of 1999, GE's stock was up 86% over a five-year period making it the most valuable company on earth, with a total market capitalization of $157 billion. And with

Exhibit 1.1
Three Levels of Performance Measures

Level/ Outcomes	Objectives	Design	Measurement Perspective
Organization	• The overarching strategy • The value migration • Organizational alignment • The business plan	• Strategy-driven functions • EVA or CVA value of functions • Permeability of boundaries • ABC/ABM-driven	• Financial perspective • Customer perspective • Organizational perspective • Operations perspective • Growth & innovation
Process	• Conformance to customer standards	• Process owner • Inputs • Outputs • Service level agreements • Boundary crossings	• Cost • Cycle time • Quantity • Quality • Conformance to standards
Job	• Report cards • Easy access • Motivation • Selection	• Process maps • Function charts • Task analysis	• Activities • Outcomes • Target measures • Data sources

earnings expected to hit $7.4 billion in the year 2000, it is poised to become America's most profitable company. What is GE doing right? Over a decade ago, GE determined that its business strategy was to be a product-focused company.

With the strong backing of its management, GE set out to differentiate itself from industry competitors by producing extremely high-quality durable products and establishing a strong product image. The entire company was oriented toward implementing that strategy. By the Fall of 1995, GE began to face slower domestic growth and cutthroat pricing abroad for its big-ticket manufacturing items. GE responded by choosing another strategy—being customer-focused—and began transforming itself into a service-oriented company, from servicing hospital equipment, locomotives and jet engines to management consulting. Today, nearly 60% of GE's profits come from services, up from 16.4% in 1980.

What GE accomplished is extraordinary, but other companies also became leaders in their industries by selecting a strategic focus and implementing it through the discipline of alignment. Strategic focus directs how a company will deploy resources. The strategic focus is the criterion against which all activity within a company should be tested. There are three basic business strategic focuses: (1) cost-focused, (2) product-focused, and (3) customer-focused.

Cost-Focused Strategy. The cost leader strategic focus is directed at producing the least costly goods and services within a specific industry. A company must command prices that are lower but close to the industry's averages, while producing goods and services well below industry costs and equal to industry quality standards. No single way to achieve this strategic focus exists, and maintaining it requires iron discipline. The most common methods for achieving this strategy are the reduction of key processes' cycle time; reduction in fully-loaded labor cost; activity-based management; and saturation of the market with standard products. Wal-Mart, GEICO, and the former U.S. Healthcare are examples of companies following a cost leader strategy.

Product-Focused Strategy. The product-focused strategy differentiates products and services along specific criteria that provide customers with unique, value-added features sold at a premium price. This means filling a niche not served by the cost leaders. The costs of products and services are still relatively important, and costs to the customer must be within one standard deviation of industry averages. Successful market-focused companies reduce the cost of any activities that don't affect their products' and services' unique qualities. Tactics for implementing this strategy include: better customer service, better distribution channels, and customization of products and services, availability of parts, and product/service image. Merck, JP Morgan and Hewlett-Packard are examples of companies following a product-focused strategy.

Customer-Focused Strategy. This strategy also involves differentiating products/services that provide customers with unique, value-added features sold at a premium price and filling a niche not served by the cost leaders. Nordstrom is the epitome of a customer-focused strategy: it offers fewer goods than other retailers but provides customers with the highest levels of service in the retail industry. Customers expect to pay a premium for that service.

Corporate Initiatives

Corporate initiatives are imposed either externally (e.g., regulations of a government agency) or internally (policies handed down by senior management). They require that a process or policy either change or be scrapped for a new one. Corporate initiatives, therefore, compete with other priorities for capital resources. Since these initiatives also affect performance, companies must implement measures that influence behavioral changes to fulfill the mandate. Most corporate initiatives are short-lived, because they are designed and implemented to close a very specific gap in a company's performance. Unfortunately, corporate initiatives often fail, because senior management doesn't develop or incorporate performance measures to hold managers accountable for implementing and sustaining the corporate initiatives.

Balanced (Corporate) Scorecards

We've seen that a strategy plus alignment management is necessary to achieve high levels of success. A third key component is to measure the critical things a company does in multiple ways. The balanced scorecard (sometimes called the corporate scorecard), is a relative newcomer to the business world. The corporate scorecard is the grouping of the major categories of key performance measures. This grouping can include financial, customer, organizational, technology and innovation, or operational key performance measures. Corporate scorecards became popular as managers increasingly realized the limitations of traditional financial performance measures. In business, most financial measures are trailing or historical (statistically, dependent variables). Most companies typically look only at financial results to measure performance. But top performing firms today use a *balanced* set of key performance measures.

Key performance measures guide both management and employees in their effort to increase customer satisfaction and shareholder value. The purpose of corporate scorecard is to communicate strategic direction; establish performance categories, baselines and targets; identify which business processes directly impact cash flow; and provide the links between strategy, the business plan, and employees' activities. Corporate scorecards are often inter-related and must be in harmony with each other. A company cannot forsake research and development and customer satisfaction for the sake of quarterly profits and expect to exist as a growing concern.

Companies that focus only on financial performance measures constantly look over their shoulders, examining past performance, which is over and done. Corporate scorecards, on the other hand, include both leading and trailing performance measures. Trailing measures (statistically, dependent variables) generally include all of the financial performance measures. Leading performance measures (statistically, independent variables) might include customer satisfaction, productivity, growth and innovation, and human resource management performance measures. Leading measures can be manipulated to affect financial results.

The next section briefly examines the five major categories of key performance measures. It is important to note that the actual categories of measures used are situational and, therefore, may be quite different than the categories presented in Kaplan's book on the balanced scorecard.

Financial Perspective. Financial results are critical of course, but what are the most important financial measures? Cash flow is the vital sign of a company, according to Jack Welch, CEO of GE. Many economists would agree, arguing that increased cash flow directly results from tapping the needs of the market. Following are some of the most common old and new financial key performance measures. Note the absence of profit as a key performance measure—profit is important, but a company may go broke if managers chase it. Many companies would be better off if managers focused greater attention on the acquisition and retention of customers, the source of all profit, than forever wondering why they didn't make their margin numbers.

Customer Perspective. Customer satisfaction is at or near the top of leading companies' key performance measures. The acquisition and retention of customers is the key to making money. Customer satisfaction is defined on a company-by-company basis. At McDonald's, which manages by a low-cost leader strategy, it means spending as little time as possible with the customer, i.e. quick service. At Nordstrom, which manages by using a customer focus strategy, it means being empathetic with the customer, i.e., high-quality service.

Previously, companies were satisfied if their phones were answered within three rings. While this is an objective performance measure, it adds little to the acquisition and retention of customers. More information about customers and their needs have led to more reliance on measuring customers' perceptions of the products and services the company provides, and how the customer are treated. These measures can make or break a company. A gap always exists between customers' expectations and their perception about the value of the products or services provided. Employees with customer contact must be educated to manage that gap, and management must be held accountable for closing it.

Operations Perspective. Productivity performance measures have changed considerably over the last 20 years. Traditionally, productivity performance measures focused on input/output ratios, counts (productivity quotas), and machine utilization. Today, the productivity focus has migrated toward tracking total process costs, process cycle time, and process setup time. Speed is the key. The speed of productivity has increased as the number of organizational layers has decreased, both made possible by the reduction of non-value–added work; the empowering of employees to assume work previously done by managers; and the development of extensive performance measurement systems.

Organizational Perspective. Past measures of organizational effectiveness focused on employee satisfaction. But recent research indicates that employees are primarily motivated by having control over their work, having greater contact with customers, and having sufficient resources to accomplish their work. Thus, the focus of employee satisfaction has shifted from the employee to managerial and organizational effectiveness. Effective managers link these key performance measures to organizational effectiveness:

- Trustworthy communication
- Availability of resources
- Availability of technology
- Proper use of employees' skills
- Respectful treatment of employees
- Successful teamwork
- Shared knowledge of strategic goals
- Leadership skills
- Shared commitment to company's values

The Activity-Based Business Plan

Once key performance measures and a corporate scorecard are created, a business plan must be developed. The business plan is the tool that links employees to the strategy and key performance measures. Its purpose is to close the gap between where the company is now (given its corporate scorecard score), and where management wants it to be next year. Business plans should be developed so that each gap-closing objective and activity has a "line-of-sight" connection to the strategy, the customer, or some key performance measure.

Many companies (including Hewlett-Packard, Eaton, Texas Instruments, and Intel) have adopted an activity-based approach to developing their business plans. Activity-based business planning identifies the activities (objectives or action steps) to be performed, the outcomes, goods and services that results from that activity, the targets of performance for both the activity and deliverable, the data source, and the time frame. Each activity is assigned to an individual who is held accountable for its achievement. This activity-based approach to business planning encourages a dialogue between management and employees about how activities and results tie to the business strategy. It also provides more useful information to employees, which means they are more likely to achieve objectives. Activity-based consultants have a saying: "It's not the form, stupid!" In other words, they believe it is more important to understand and implement the activity-based concept than to be concerned about the appearance of the written document.

Process Performance Measures

Managers need to measure how well their companies' processes are actually working. Company leaders have eliminated many layers of management over the last 10 years and given ownership of all processes to those running them. These leaders have mapped every key process and incorporated performance measures covering cost, cycle time, conformance to customer standards, quantity, and quality into each activity.

Process mapping, a technique familiar to those involved in total quality management, is a graphic depiction of the activities performed in a process. Many businesses now have flow charts, one form of process mapping. Process maps have the advantage of accomplishing many tasks using one method, and in the long run they are more cost-beneficial than many other methods of gathering performance data.

Process maps usually show the amount of time and resources (labor, overhead, allocation distributions, depreciation, etc.) it takes to perform each activity. All of the activities that do not add customer value or are not aligned with the business strategy are eliminated, thus eliminating the number of boundary crossings between jobs or departments. The map is then reconstructed; noting any cost savings and cycle time reductions achieved in the improved version. Process maps invariably identify processes that can be simplified, automated or eliminated, and they help improve hand-offs between customers and employees. This reduces error and cycle time and increases productivity. Once the map is completed, performance measures for each activity (duty, task, action steps) can be developed and implemented in employees' performance profiles. A word of caution: many performance measurement teams are under unrealistic pressure to develop and implement a performance measurement system. Developing process maps can be very time consuming.

Developing Job Performance Measures

Job-level performance measures can be developed directly from process maps, but in many cases process maps do not exist or there are time constraints in developing performance measures. Therefore, at the job level, there are basic methods of identifying activities and developing performance measures: process maps, task analysis, function charts, and group interviews.

Process Maps. Process maps are excellent data sources for individual performance measures. Once the tasks in a process map identify performance measures for customers, quality, quantity, cycle time, and costs can be generated. Exhibit 1.2 represents a 1-800 Telephony Sales Process map. This map shows the complete customer ordering process at the major activity levels.

Task Analysis. Task analysis simply asks employees which tasks they perform. Task data are often given individual numbers and stored in a database with demographic information such as name, immediate supervisor, and department. This process simplifies record-keeping and standardizes tasks and their names. Using a database also allows

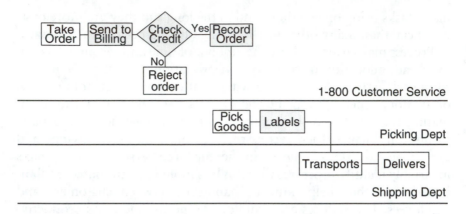

Exhibit 1.2. A Customer Order Process

employees and managers to look at performance close to real time detail, thereby decreasing the time it takes to solve a problem.

Function charts. Function charts provide the most detail for any job. They list all the major activities performed in a process down the left column, as is done in Exhibit 1.3. Next, all the people, organizations, or systems are listed across the top row. At the intersection of an activity and a contact, the specific activity at that intersection is noted.

Group Interviews. Through structured group interviews, generally referred to as focus groups or nominal group technique (NGT), a wide variety of information is obtained in a relatively brief time. An NGT engages several individuals at one time, generates many ideas, eliminates redundancies, and gets consensus on the most important ideas through a voting procedure. In short, it allows a team to cover many jobs and many employees in the shortest possible time, while providing a relatively safe level of reliability and validity.

The Individual Performance Profile

Many managers strive for the companies' employees to be accountable to the overall business plan. A few have managed to succeed through the use of the individual performance profile. This profile is based on the trend among top companies to use a more comprehensive method of measuring performance, known as "activity-based management profiles." Profiles must include activities, the deliverables resulting

Exhibit 1.3
Payroll Information Function Chart Example

Dependencies/Tasks	Customer (Employee)	Sales Screen Order	PeopleSoft Comp	Expert Advisor
Benefits Consulting	• take customer order	• use to verify address, mail code, and any personal info. • used to confirm process dates and info (pay, and personal, org, CC) changed on profile (history)	• used to view paychecks and various deductions • used to look at history of ee's benefits (date changes and status changes) • used to view current selection of benefits • used to view COBRA	• document calls, • confirm history of calls, • used to transfer items that need to be researched • used to log in forms and checks
Payroll Consulting	• provide customer service regarding their pay questions	• used to confirm process dates of info (pay, and personal, org, CC) changed on profile (history)	• used to verify salary YTD • used to view paychecks and various deductions • used to determine if group benefits were deducted correctly • used to view damaged check reprints • verify awards and amounts and what CC used	• document calls, • confirm history of calls, • used to transfer items that need to be researched
HR Policy/Procedure Consulting	• provide customer service regarding their policy and procedure questions	• use to verify HR data		• document calls, • confirm history of calls, • used to transfer items that need to be researched
Call Distribution/ Call Directing		• document calls, • confirm history of calls, • used to transfer items that need to be researched	• used to keep team informed of any communications regarding problems, concerns, issues, and general information	
Severance Lump Sum Processing	• provide customer service regarding employee's lump sum questions	• use to verify address and any personal info, service dates and retirement eligibility	• used to verify if/when lump sum check is issued	• used to document lump sum form rec'd and severance info

from those activities, the targets of performance, data sources, and due dates. The purpose of the profile is to:

- Align all activity with the business plan or strategy
- Measure employee performance against a balanced scorecard
- Use one document for performance assessment and wage administration
- Provide a common framework for assessing many incumbents occupying the same job
- Increase the dialogue surrounding individual contributions to the business while reducing the overall amount of time spent on performance assessment

Frequently Asked Questions About Performance Measurement

What are key performance measures? Key performance measures are the major trailing and leading measures in the corporate scorecard. They include financials, customer satisfaction, growth and innovation, organizational effectiveness, and productivity. Under the customer satisfaction category, performance measures might include retention, acquisition, empathy, reliability, business knowledge, and aesthetics.

Who is responsible for performance measures? Management owns the performance measurement system and is responsible for setting key performance measures. Department heads are responsible for setting departmental measures and process measures. Employees are responsible for helping management develop performance measures at all levels. In leading companies, managers are held accountable for implementing the business strategy, and the performance measurement system is the system that measures the success of their implementation. This is all the more reason that performance measures must support the business strategy.

Why aren't financial results a sufficient measure of company performance? Performance measures are divided into to two basic types: trailing and leading.

- **Trailing performance measures** are historical in nature and only provide a view of the organization's past performance. Financial performance measures (with the exception of cash flow) are examples of trailing performance measures.

- **Leading performance measures** are increasingly more important, because they act as an early warning system. They indicate, in advance, potential success or failure. Examples of leading performance measures categories are customer satisfaction and human resource management. In short, you can't manage results, but you can manage the activities that lead to success.

How long should it take to develop and implement performance measures? Management often asks a performance measurement team to develop and implement performance measures within 90 days. That's an impossible task. It takes leading managers years to develop and perfect their systems. It took Merck 14 years to settle on 18 key performance measures in its balanced scorecard and chances are very good that four or five of those measures will change in the next 18 months. A minimum of two years should be allotted to designing and implementing a performance measurement project. There is a rule among performance measurement consultants: for every hour you spend collecting performance measures for the project, you will spend five hours revising, getting approval, and implementing them.

How many performance measures are enough? Most departments only need between five and 10 performance measures that capture 80% of the work done in the department. Using a balanced scorecard approach will increase the coverage of work done by all departments. Individuals need to be held accountable for two or more objectives from the business plan as well as five to 10 performance measures that cover their routine operations.

Why are we being measured against things we cannot control? Current thinking about performance measures stresses the importance of holding all employees accountable, to some extent, for the overall financial results of the company or business unit. In many companies all employees are held accountable for at least 10% of the overall company results in order to make employees more aware of their contribution to the success or failure of the company. But using weightings factors in the extent of direct control over financial measures. Secretaries are often held accountable for the way they manage supply expenses. But their overall effect on financial results is minimal, and, therefore, their contribution may be weighted at 15%.

How do we establish standards and weights for performance measures? Performance standards are developed based on cycle time, costs, conformance to customer standards, quantity and quality. Weights are established based on the needs of your business. Greater need should lead to greater weights.

How often and where do we get the data for performance measures? Gathering performance data depends on the needs of the business. If a job can be completed in a short amount of time, perhaps a weekly sampling of performance data would suffice. The end of major projects would be a good time to collect performance data.

Why should we spend time developing performance measures when we have work to do? Performance measures act as a compass; help set direction; focus efforts on critical activities; provide data to improve performance; and align all activities, tasks, and results with organization goals. To accomplish this, managers in world-class businesses spend 50% of their time gathering performance information. Further, many of these managers measure how well they develop their performance measurement system. To demonstrate the importance of performance measures, some firms' policies state that managers can only receive compensation equivalent to their performance measurement skills.

How do we reconcile a delay in our performance measures? Some of the work we do today does not impact the bottom line for several years. The use of leading performance measures helps this by focusing attention on doing the right things, which leads to getting the right results.

What can we do to improve results when they are out of synch with the standards? Go to management and explain to them what you see as the problem, but go with some facts and figures to present your case. Arm yourself with performance data. Having one or more solutions is much more likely to get you a fair hearing.

Summary

1) Top managers adopt a well-defined and communicated business strategy with a specific focus.

2) There are three core strategic focuses:
   a) Cost focus
   b) Service focus
   c) Product focus

3) Top managers adopt a specific set (more than 10, less than 30) of key performance measures (a balanced scorecard) covering a diverse set of performance categories (e.g., employee satisfaction, customer satisfaction, productivity, growth and innovation, financial results).
   a) The purpose of balanced (corporate) scorecard is to communicate strategic direction; establish performance categories, baselines and targets; identify which business processes directly impact cash flow; and provide the links between strategy, the business plan, and employees' activities.

4) Top managers close gaps between organization, technology, and process architectures. Closely aligning each element, within each architecture, greatly enhances company performance.

5) Top managers align all the activities from top to bottom within the organization. If an activity doesn't add value, managers outsource or eliminate it.

6) Top managers have control over processes.
   a) The assigned ownership of processes to specific individuals or groups.
   b) They develop cost, cycle time, conformance to standards, quantity and quality target measures.

7) Top managers develop individual performance profiles that:
   a) Align all activity with the business plan or strategy.
   b) Measure employee performance against a balanced scorecard.
   c) Provide a common framework for assessing many incumbents occupying the same job.
   d) Increase the dialogue surrounding individual contributions to the business while reducing the overall amount of time spent in performance assessment.

8) Top managers hold their direct reports accountable for building and using focused strategies, scorecards, process measures, and individual performance profiles.

Endnotes

1. Porter, Michael, *Competitive Strategy: Techniques for Analyzing Industries and Competitors.* New York: The Free Press, 1980.
   – Porter, Michael, *Competitive Advantage: Creating and Sustaining Superior Performance.* New York: The Free Press, 1985.
   – Porter, Michael, "What Is Strategy?" *The Harvard Business Review*, November–December 1996, pp. 61–78.

2. Kaplan, Robert S., and Norton, David P. *The Balanced Scorecard. Translating Strategy into Action.* Boston: Harvard Business Press, 1996.

3. In statistics, independent variables are changed or manipulated in order to affect a change on a dependent variable. The temperature of yeast in bread making is the independent variable; changing the temperature of the yeast changes the texture of the bread. In business, customer satisfaction is an independent variable. Increasing customer satisfaction increases profit, the dependent variable.

The Strategic Focus: The Context for All Performance Measures

2

What is a strategic focus? All managers can describe a strategic plan. But very few managers can describe strategic focus, and indicate whether their company has one.[1] To an increasing number of managers, strategy means "the plan" (goals, targets, objectives, action steps, etc.) needed to achieve the financial goals of the company. Several studies conducted over the last five years show that reengineering, TQM, downsizing, and other initiatives largely have failed![2] Only a handful of the many companies, which undertook these initiatives, improved their financial position. Why? Because the initiatives were implemented without a context, and companies did not relate them to a strategic focus.

Most companies don't have a strategic focus, and many would argue against its importance. In the late 1980s, many managers were convinced that the pace of change would make any strategy obsolete in less than a year. This is a basic misunderstanding of the difference between strategic focus and a strategic plan. But, there is swing back to strategy again, which is best demonstrated by the August 26, 1996 cover of *Business Week,* "Strategy is Back!"[3]

Strategic focus is the central business thesis that extends over and throughout the company. It is the guiding principle that differentiates one company from another. *It is the primary focus of the company.* The reasoning is simple and straightforward; a strategic focus:

- Drives the way the company will market its product and services
- Determines how the company allocates resources
- Sets the context for everything from performance measures to corporate-wide initiatives

Strategic focus is also a public statement that says, "We offer this product or service at this price, with this kind of service, and we will stake our reputation on it!" It's the difference between the way Wal-Mart and Nordstrom make money. Finally, strategic focus is the first and most important performance criterion, the measure of all other measures, against which all business decisions should be examined.

Michael Porter first stated the importance of developing a market-oriented strategy in the early eighties.[4] Porter's work has been revised and extensively adapted since the 1980s.[5]

In the *Discipline of Market Leaders,* Michael Treacy and Fred Wiersama streamline Porter's arguments for implementing either a low-cost or differentiating strategy.[6] They called their focused strategies "value disciplines." Similarly, other authors have found three main, but generic strategies, which will be referred to as strategic focuses. They are:

1. **Cost-focused.** A low-cost leader provides a standard product at the lowest cost to its customers. Also, the company provides a standard product at an average price but with the lowest internal production costs. This focus is driven by operational excellence.
2. **Product-focused.** A product-focused strategy specializes in providing niche products or services that are not provided by the low-cost leader. Having new products in the pipeline at all times drives this focus.
3. **Customer-focused.** All companies have to have basic, competent customer service, just to survive. However, customer focused companies differentiate themselves by providing world-class, exceptional service to their customers. Many companies claim to have world-class customer service, but the number of companies that actually provide this can be counted on both hands.

Why Only One of Three Strategy Focuses?

Only three strategy focuses sounds too limiting. But there are thousands of possible permutations. For example, L.L. Bean and Nordstrom both have world-class customer service. L.L. Bean provides "no-questions-asked" return for problem products but makes its margins on volume. Nordstrom makes its profit on the markups of upscale items. Southwest Airlines and Wal-Mart are two more cost-focused companies, but management is very different from that at L.L. Bean and Nordstrom. No single company can excel at being a cost-leader, product-focused, and customer-focused over the long term without significantly reducing its margins or raising its prices. There is always tension over simultaneously managing conflicting concerns. To be a cost leader necessarily means that the *focus* for that company is delivering its products or services for the least amount of cost to themselves and their customers. This means fewer resources can be allocated to either customer service or product development.

In 1980 during a business conference, Peter Drucker spoke about strategic focus. He used a simple triangle to explain why companies cannot be all things to all people and still make money. The analogy is not perfect but it does work well as a symbol for understanding the concept of strategic focus.

Imagine the triangle in Exhibit 2.1 has sides of equal length representing the way a company focuses its attention and resources. The company pays equal attention to costs, products, and service.

Suppose a company decides to change from being all-things-to-all-people and focuses on the development of niche products as a strategic focus. What would the triangle look like?

Granted, the strategic triangle is simple. But it does help illustrate how the tension among costs, service, and products drives the degree to which managers can focus their attention or make resource allocation decisions. For example, a cost leader can't ignore customer service completely without losing some of its customer base. To be successful, all companies have to be good at service, and provide the goods and services that people want in their niche. From a cost point of view, none of

Exhibit 2.1 The All-Things-to-All-People Strategic Focus

them can be more than one standard deviation from the average price for a specific product or service and expect to compete.

Of course, there are infinite variations on the three basic strategies, with each variation being driven by the core competencies of each company.[7] Research and best practices clearly suggest that the farther a company deviates from a strategic focus and its core competencies, the more difficult it becomes to sustain profits and growth over the long term.

Strategic focus is also about making choices and having the discipline to stick to them. Choices like Southwest Airlines "no meals, no baggage transfers, no travel agents" is part of its low-cost strategy. Pfizer's refusal to follow all the other major pharmaceuticals into the low cost generic market is another example. Pfizer is a product-focused company and is betting that its concentration on the development of new products will provide a double-digit return on its investments. We have more detailed descriptions of the three focused strategies with examples of companies using each.

The Cost Leader

Southwest Airlines and Wal-Mart are America's favorite cost leaders. Southwest Airlines is the most profitable airline in the air. It is famous for quick turnaround times, high plane utilization, and limited customer service. Its employees are the most satisfied among all companies in the United States and some of the highest paid in the industry. Wal-Mart is famous for developing and maintaining the best (the fastest and the cheapest) distribution channel in the retail business. This reliance on superior distribution channels, along with its legendary full court vendor press, has assured it top 10 ratings over a number of years. GEICO has long been known as a cost leader of insurance products. GEICO gets its pre-eminence from streamlined processes and the lowest cost per employee of any insurer in the business. Ikea is the world leader in modular furniture for young families on the move. In each case the company has used its core competencies to support its strategic focus and increase its margins. As a caveat, the cost leader's strategic focus is the easiest to adopt but requires the most discipline to maintain. Many cost leaders end up becoming all-things-to-all-people companies and lose their competitive edge.

The Product-Focused Strategy (Exhibit 2.2)

Pfizer is the world leader in the number and kind of successful pharmaceuticals now in the market. Pfizer steadfastly has stuck to its product development strategy and has reaped huge successes. Other pharmaceutical companies entered the low-cost generics and ended competing not only with the pharmaceutical companies manufacturing generics, but also with themselves. Johnson & Johnson is the world leader in the design, development, distribution, and sales of medical materials and equipment. Hewlett-Packard is world famous for its innovative, high quality products and can charge a premium for its personal printers, because it has the reputation for manufacturing the best. Canon and Lexmark are in continuous personal printer price wars.

Exhibit 2.2 The Product-Focused Strategy

The Customer-Focused Strategy

In this focused strategy, management emphasis is on differentiating its products and services along specific criteria that provide customers with unique, value-added features sold at a premium price. In short, charging a premium price for products allows them to provide customer service that no other company can compete with. If one had to pick the epitome of a customer-focused strategy, it would be Nordstrom. The strategy is to provide its customers with the highest levels of service in the retail industry. Customers walk into Nordstrom knowing they will pay a premium price for the goods and services offered. But Nordstrom's company culture is customer-driven and, therefore, overcomes price resistance. Home Depot hires, trains and measures the ability of their sales associates to answer questions on everything from screwdrivers costing $2.70 to fanciful doors costing $2,700.

Key Performance Measures of Three Strategy Focuses

Each strategic focus has different assumptions about future performance measures. Exhibit 2.3 reveals the major attributes of each strategic focus. While these attributes are often associated with a particular strategy there is often a considerable amount of overlap.

Exhibit 2.3
Key Performance Measures of Focused Strategies

Cost-Focused	Product-Focused	Service-Focused
Core competencies (e.g., distribution channels) are the competitive advantage. Always cost and efficiency driven.	Focuses on the development of new products designed to fill specific niches not filled by the cost leaders.	The focus is on the customer, the relationship. Customer intimacy is at the core of this strategy.
Performance Measures: • Cost • Cycle time • Conformance to standards • Quantity • Quality	Performance Measures: • Number of new products in the pipeline • R&D budget • Time to Market • Customization • Field service expertise • Flexible technology • Employee satisfaction	Performance Measures: • Appearances • Complaint handling • Customer empathy • Customer intimacy • Customer-based technology • Limited number of supported products • Product knowledge • Responsiveness

Key performance measures of cost leader-focused strategies

Costs. In order to maintain a cost leader strategy, production and delivery costs must be held to a minimum while maintaining high levels of quality. Cost leaders focus on the total throughputs for specific process, not just the overall costs. Basic sub-measures include the reduction of waste and the length of time from order input to delivery.

Cycle Time. Cycle time is the heart of all productivity gains. When Motorola implemented its cycle time reduction projects, the results were significant: manufacturing cycles times were reduced 60 to 70%; and administrative cycle times were reduced by as much as 90%. The DayCo Corporation introduced process mapping and other total quality management techniques to every employee with emphasis on eliminating any non–value-added tasks from processes.

Conformance to Standards. The ability to meet or exceed customer standards is fundamental to attracting and keeping them. But the focus is still on meeting the customers' standards. These standards have to be shared throughout the company. Nothing can be more frustrating to customers than to have one plant or department blame another for not meeting its standards.

Quantity. Low-cost leaders make their margins on large quantities. Therefore, low-cost leaders are constantly examining ways they can increase quantity without increasing costs. In the late 1980s, National Can was happy if it produced 1,000 beer cans a minute. Today, it uses ceramic cutters and folders which can withstand the heat generated in high-speed production and can produce over 2,000 beer cans a minute.

Quality. Product reliability is at the heart of all contemporary companies. Building reliable products increases customer loyalty and reduces material waste and employee time spent on repairs. Intel, Hewlett-Packard, and Motorola are successful because each company's management believes product reliability is the single best way to win and retain customers. As Phil Crosby said, "Quality is free!" With TQM and six sigma projects still under full steam, quality will be at the heart of every successful company. This applies equally well to service companies. Rework in service companies is often very high. Focusing attention on getting things done right, the first time, is essential to long term growth.

Is operational excellence the same as low-cost strategy?

All companies must pay close attention to "operational excellence" if they want to remain competitive. *But being internally efficient and effective is* not *a strategy.* Here is why. First, customers don't care if a company is operationally excellent. And why should they? Customers care about these questions:

- Can I afford this product?
- Do I want these product features?
- What kind of customer service can I expect?

Second, operational excellence is internally focused. This is necessry but insufficient to drive success. Third, all operational improvements are curvilinear: at some point improvement reaches a plateau beyond which further improvements are either impossible or not cost efficient. When that plateau is reached, there needs to be a strategic focus to drive the company forward.

Key performance measures of product-focused strategies

Number of new products in the pipeline. New products in the computer technology industry have a competitive advantage of a year or less. In the pharmaceutical industry, the average development time is between 8 and 12 years. Success in both industries is dependent on having viable new products in the pipeline.

R&D/Total budget. Product-focused companies must keep their new product pipeline filled to capacity. New products require research and development. The most successful companies using a product-focused strategy have greater percentages of their total budgets allocated to research and development than do less successful companies.

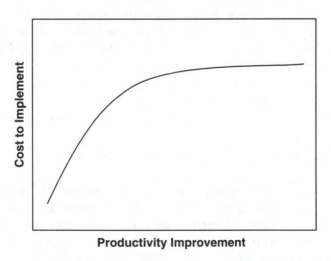

Productivity Improvement

Exhibit 2.4
Productivity Life Cycle

Time to market. This is a variation on the "new-products-in-the-pipeline" measure. Companies that are first with a new product on the market usually are the winners. Reducing development cycle time is now the driving force of all product-focused companies. This last measure is largely dependent upon management's ability to integrate both design and manufacturing technologies, as well as design and manufacturing personnel. An important sub-measure would be cross-functional cooperation.

Customer-driven customization. The most successful product focused-companies, (HP, Levi) have computer-driven, cost effective manufacturing plants with the capability of producing lot sizes of one. For example, Levi's private label jeans are custom measured for each individual. The measurements are sent by computer to the manufacturing plant, where the custom jeans just become part of the overall manufacturing process. The customer pays a 20% premium to purchase these jeans, but the custom jeans add no cost for Levi.

Field service representatives expertise. Product-focused leaders know that they can live or die by the level and expertise of their field service representatives. Therefore, it is imperative to get the field service representatives involved in soliciting and providing performance data about products and service. GE management is legendary in providing its field representatives with the latest and greatest in technological help. This company was among the first to put service manuals on CD-ROMs and provide its representatives with sophisticated laptop computers, reducing the amount of down time walking to and from service vehicles to retrieve the manuals. Both clients and representatives were delighted.

Employee-centered. The most successful product-focused managers make the most use of their employees. Turnover becomes an increasingly important performance measure. The reason is simple: employee turnover affects the core competency of the organization. If turnover is exceptionally high, employees spend a considerable amount of time engaged in relearning, and reducing responsiveness.

Key performance measures of customer-focused strategies

Appearances. Customers willing to pay a premium for world-class service demand that employees are well groomed and facilities are attractive. Appearances include the proper use of language.

Complaint handling. A key success factor for customer-focused companies is the means of handling customer complaints. Customer-focused companies earn premium prices for their goods and services. If they have problems, customers expect the company to handle them with the least amount of inconvenience. That is why Nordstrom authorizes each of its employees to settle customer complaints without the need for supervisory approval, for up to $2,000. L.L. Bean's no hassle complaint-handling policy also is famous around the world.

Customer empathy/intimacy. Demonstrating an understanding of the issues and desires of the customer are at the heart of a service-focused company. The nod of the head, the pregnant pause, the probing question, the *"Gee, I bet that made you feel . . ."* signal that the customer is with someone who cares about him or her. In most world-class service companies, phone encounters with customers are scripted. Before first contact is made with customers, employees are intensely trained in the art of empathy.

Customer-based technology and customer intimacy. The goal of any customer-focused company is to be the sole provider of a given set of products or services. To accomplish this, customer-focused companies maintain *extensive customer data warehouses,* including the customers' likes and dislikes, their spouses' and children's names, pets' names, birthdays, anniversaries, color and style preferences, etc. With this extensive amount of data comes the increasing responsibility not to share it with any other company. In essence, a bond develops between the customer and the company that includes openly agreed upon statements about whether the customer's data will be shared.

Knowledge of products and services. Customer-focused companies limit the number of products they offer to their customers. Offering fewer products requires less capital expenditure for the purchase of goods and warehousing. Further, fewer products make it much more likely that employees will be able to discuss intelligently all aspects of the products and services provided. However, the company must allocate enough resources so the employees that interact with customers can answer all questions or solve most problems.

Responsiveness. Customer-focused companies must be willing to "jump through any number of hoops" to satisfy individual customer needs. For affluent customers, this may be picking them up at home in a limousine or having goods delivered. It may mean going to extraordinary lengths to find a specific color the customer wants in a dress or a suit. For premium service, companies' personal shoppers are typical.

What are the downsides of not implementing a strategic focus?

There are other alternatives besides adopting a strategic focus. Most often, it is the all-things-to-all-people strategy. This strategy forces companies into the less profitable world of hyper-competition with other all-things-to-all-people companies. The moral is that having the discipline to establish and maintain a strategic focus leads to long-term financial success, even in competitive markets. In the end, the all-things-to-all-people strategy costs the company its focus; reduces its ability to be a leader within the industry; and decreases its return on shareholder equity. When a company does not develop and implement a strategic focus, the following are often the outcome.

- Tries to be all-things-to-all-people
- Forces managers to focus on the financial results while ignoring customer acquisition and retention, R&D expenditures, and improving internal processes
- Drives up the cost of overhead in maintaining complex and custom systems needed to meet the customer's needs
- Forces companies to compete heavily for customers that are themselves less than successful. In short, competing for low margin customers
- Causes confusion among customers and Wall Street analysts trying to understand the company's direction

Mixed Strategies

Using mixed strategies is less common but can be as successful as the other three, providing companies work under some constraints. Mixed strategies often are used in large corporations that supply products and services to many different markets or work in many industries. Some products and services use a lost cost leader approach in one industry while using a customer or product-focused approach in another. For example, GE has a product or customer focus in all its industries except home electronics, where RCA and GE are marketed alongside Samsung and other cost leaders. Like the cost strategy, using mixed strategies requires discipline to avoid becoming all-things-to-all-people. A mixed strategy will not work in companies in which there are competing strategic focuses within the same unit. For example, American Airlines tried to compete with Southwest Airlines and lost. The divergence between the service orientation and cost orientation was too great to overcome.

Switching Strategies

Switching strategies is not a common practice. The reasons are simple and straightforward. First, large-scale organizational change within a company is always difficult to accomplish. It is even more difficult when the change involves customer or Wall Street perceptions. In the following way we address some change strategies and the results for some companies:

From a cost leader to any other strategy. There are very few companies that have switched from a low-cost leader strategy to another successfully. Border's Book and Music and Sports Authority found it difficult to be successful mid-scale marketers because of the cost leader image of K-Mart. Once these companies were spun from K-Mart, financial success was quick to follow. Customers are skeptical of companies that switch strategies. Customers choose cost leaders' products and services, because dollar value is important to them. Wall Street is seldom convinced that large scale organizational change is even possible. The most successful companies to make the switch have been American Honda, Toyota, and J.C. Penney. It took the Japanese car makers from the late 1960s to the early 1980s to shake their image of producers of low-cost, low-quality vehicles. It has taken J.C. Penney 15 years to shed its image of purveyor of low-cost goods to become America's favorite department store.

From a product- or customer-focused strategy to a low-cost leader. Moving from a product- or customer-focused strategy to a cost leader is the easiest strategy change to accomplish. It requires nerves of steel and discipline, but the change can revitalize a company. Dwindling loyalty in the consumer products industry led Proctor and Gamble to switch from a premium product strategy to a cost strategy. The company greatly reduced the number of products it manufactures and increased its margins. Return on equity rose 40%. The conglomerates of the 1980s are becoming the more focused companies of the twenty-first century. AT&T spun Lucent Technologies, and Pepsi sold its restaurant business to focus on snack food and soft drinks.

The Importance of Alignment Management

All organizations, whether they be *Fortune 500* conglomerates or mom and pop family companies, are composed of three distinct architectures: technology, organization, and processes.

Technology Architecture. Technology architecture is the information management system which delivers the data employees need to make decisions; the production/operations technology that is instrumental in delivering core product/service; and other software applications.

Organizational Architecture. The organization architecture is an organization's culture (prevalent values, beliefs, assumptions); the administrative policies that drive behavior; business systems (e.g., planning, budgeting); human resource systems (everything from recruiting and rewards to succession planning); the knowledge, skills, and abilities of the workforce; and the organization's structure (job design, reporting relationships, staffing levels).

Process Architecture. Process architecture is the business process and physical layout of work areas. Whenever any part of one architecture is changed, ripple effects occur in the other architectures. For example, when a process is modified it will likely impact the IT technology, HR systems, performance metrics, job design, and physical layout. The final point is that the strategy should drive the configuration of the architectures, not the other way around.

Discipline and Alignment Management

The connection between discipline and success is recognized more now than at any other time since the emergence of the post-industrial era. It is not mere coincidence that the top 10 most successful companies in the United States are also the most disciplined companies. It is impossible to separate alignment management and discipline. Alignment management is a very powerful tool to help companies maintain the strategic discipline. Discipline often means ending relationships with unprofitable customers. You will not be able to support some customers, because the amount of capital resources required exceeds the returns that the customer provides.

Once or twice a year, property and casualty insurance companies ask their local offices to "clean their books." This is a pleasant sounding way of telling customers that their policies have been canceled, largely because the risks were too high or the cost too great to the insurer. While home and car owners may have some recourse within some states, commercial enterprises seldom do. Getting new insurance after cancellation is often very difficult and expensive. There are potential complaints to the state insurance commissioner, lawsuits, and damage to the company's reputation. But, in order to be successful, insurance companies must be disciplined and cleanse their books of bad customers. Smart insurance companies understand the reluctance their managers have to do this. To help, they develop retention ratios for each local office, based on the quality and quantity of customers on their books.

How do companies get their managers to implement and maintain a strategy? Most of them ensure that performance measures are aligned from the strategy to the job on the factory floor. The strategy drives the performance measures used in the balanced scorecard or other set of corporate-wide key performance measures. This then cascades to the business plan, process measures, service level agreements, and individual performance measures.

Often a common set of performance measures are used throughout the company, with special emphasis on those measures that most support the focused strategy. Aetna, Inc.'s Corporate Human Resources oversees and manages the company's benefits and payroll, a $2 billion operation. Corporate Human Resources has a balanced scorecard, and a set of five measures from this scorecard are part of everyone's performance profile (read performance appraisal form). Further, each person in Corporate Human Resources is held responsible for one or more business objectives. Finally, each person has a list of activities, outcomes, and target measures covering his or her job and for which he or she is responsible. This completes the link from the strategy to the person.

Mission or vision statements are the single most expansive and carefully crafted statement of an organization's direction. However, one mission statement looks just like any other mission statement. Often such statements are too basic to be useful and often contradictory in terms of strategy. Here is a generic example:

The XYZ Corporation will become the low-cost choice for widgets, the premier service provider, and leader in the development of new, technologically advanced widgets. We will increase growth, market share, and stockholder value, while valuing our employees and reducing costs.

Such statements defy the logic behind a strategic focus. On a flight home, a contract programmer with less than a year's experience with GE talked enthusiastically about Jack Welch's commitment to GE's new customer-focused strategy. The contract programmer was not a regular GE employee and yet was aware of GE's strategic focus. In contrast, two seats over on the same flight was a life-insurance company manager with 10 years experience. He was complaining about how he and his staff had been charged with reducing costs to a minimum and developing a dozen new products while simultaneously providing their customers with premium (i.e., Nordstrom-like) customer service. He said it was impossible, and he could not accomplish it in the time and with the resources allotted. He was right. No company can be all-things-to-all-people, and that is exactly what his company was trying to do.

A Simple Message

Smart managers have not dispensed with mission statements, because they are useful marketing and communication tools. What smart managers do differently is:

- State their strategy publicly
- Communicate the strategy to every employee, everywhere, multiple times
- Communicate sincerity
- Hold all employees, especially management, accountable

How many times have companies promised world-class service only to leave you listening to elevator music on the phone for 10 minutes waiting for a customer service representative? Contradictory information confuses employees as well as customers. Asking employees to judge their activities against the strategic focus makes it easier for employees to relate and to remember. When choosing strategies, there are only three: cost leader, product-focused, and customer-focused.

Summary

1) Strategic focus is *the primary focus of the company*. The reasoning is simple and straightforward:

   a) a strategic focus drives the way the company will market its product and services,

   b) it determines how the company allocates resources, and sets the context for everything from performance measures to corporate-wide initiatives.

2) There are three strategic focuses:

   a) Cost-focused. A low-cost leader provides a standard product at the lowest cost to its customers. Also the company provides a standard product at an average price but with the lowest internal production costs. This focus is driven by operational excellence.

   b) Product-focused. A product-focused strategy specializes in providing niche products or services that are not provided by the low-cost leader. Having new products in the pipeline at all times drives this focus.

   c) Customer-focused. All companies have to have basic, competent customer service, just to survive. However, customer-focused companies differentiate themselves by providing world-class, exceptional service to its customers. Many companies claim to have world-class customer service, but the number of companies that actually provide this can be counted on both hands.

3) The downside of not having a strategic focus:

   a) Tries to be all-things-to-all-people

   b) Forces managers to focus on the financial results while ignoring customer acquisition and retention, R&D expenditures, and improving internal processes

   c) Drives up the cost of overhead in maintaining complex and custom systems needed to meet the customer's needs

   d) Forces companies to compete heavily for customers that are themselves less than successful. In short, competing for low margin customers

   e) Causes confusion among customers and Wall Street analysts trying to understand the company's direction.

4) All companies have three architectures:

   a) Technology Architecture. Technology architecture is the information management system which delivers the data employees need to make decisions, the production/operations technology that is instrumental in delivering core product/service, and other software applications.

   b) Organizational Architecture. The organization architecture is an organization's culture (prevalent values, beliefs, assumptions); the administrative policies that drive behavior; business systems (e.g., planning, budgeting); human resource systems (everything from recruiting and rewards to succession planning); the knowledge, skills, and abilities of the workforce; and the organization's structure (job design, reporting relationships, staffing levels).

   c) Process Architecture. Process architecture is the business process and physical layout of work areas.

5) It is impossible to separate alignment management and discipline. Discipline often means ending relationships with unprofitable customers.

Endnotes

1. Results from the Performance Measurement Questionnaire used at the beginning of every AMA Performance Measures for Your Business Workshop.

2. Hall, G., Rosenthal, J., and Wade, D. "How to Make Reengineering Work." *Harvard Business Review,* 71:6, November/December 1993, pp. 199–131.

3. Byrne, John A. "Strategic Planning." *Business Week,* August 26, 1996. pp. 46–53.

4. Porter, Michael. *Competitive Strategy: Techniques for Analyzing Industries and Competitors.* New York: The Free Press, 1980.

   Porter, Michael. *Competitive Advantage: Creating and Sustaining Superior Performance.* New York: The Free Press, 1985.

5. Treacy, M., and Wiersema, F. "How Market Leaders Keep Their Edge." *Fortune,* February 6, 1996. pp. 88–98.

   Dial, T. "Differentiate Strategies for Future Success." *Bank Management,* Sept./Oct. 1995, Vol. 71, Issue 5, pp. 20–22.

6. Nayyar, P. "On the Measurement of Competitive Strategy." Evidence from Large Multiproduct U.S. Firms.

   Academy of Management Journal, the American Management Association, December 1993, Vol. 36, Issue 6. pp. 1652–1669.

7. Hamel, Gary, and Prahalad, C. K. *Competing for the Future.* Boston: The Harvard Business School Press, 1996.

Creating and Implementing a Strategy

3

Introduction

A strategy is analogous to a map. If one is traveling to a new area, the map provides direction and plots a course from where you are to where you want to be. A well-defined and executed strategy will do the same thing.

An effective strategy must be a top down process. The process starts with the creation of an enterprise-wide strategic plan. From this plan, the Strategic Business Unit and functional strategic plans are created.

The Strategic Planning Process

Strategic planning is akin to putting together a large mosaic or puzzle. Each piece or part represents information and data. The result is a clear picture of what's happening in the external environment that positively or negatively impacts the organization. Also, the picture should depict the current level of functioning within the organization. With both perspectives, the senior management team can then chart a course for future direction.

A strategic planning process can be expeditious, easy to understand, and easy to use. The following 10 tasks, regardless of whether you are in enterprise-wide, SBU, or functional strategic planning, will help the company's management team develop a strategy:

1. Conduct current situation analysis
2. Determine planning horizon
3. Conduct environmental scan
4. Identify key success factors
5. Complete gap analysis
6. Create vision
7. Develop business strategy
8. Create balanced scorecard
9. Identify tactics and initiatives
10. Execute strategy

Task 1: Conduct Current Situation Analysis

You must recognize where you are before you determine your direction. Situation analysis creates a tangible baseline of performance. This baseline is identified by studying trends of financial performance (ROI, profit margins), operational performance (cycle times, productivity, etc.), and stakeholder perceptions (employee or customer perceptions).

An obvious question that begs to be asked is "How long is a trend?" Well, that depends on many different things, such as the planning horizon of the organization (discussed later in this chapter), the volatility of the business environment in which you compete, and the overall health of the organization. Recent trends need to be evaluated relative to longer historical performance. A stock market correction can adversely affect the stock price of a public company. It's not uncommon that within a short amount of time the stock price can reach its previous high as new buyers look for under-valued companies. Organizational performance is really a function of when you take the "snap shot" and the time period you are considering. Many of the past Baldrige award winners and companies cited for their performance in the best-selling business book, *In Search of Excellence,* fell on hard times in later years.

Other variables to consider are the interdependence and the direction of the trends being studied, and how they impact organizational performance. It's conceivable that an organization focused on cost cutting could close several field locations and layoff many employees. This would result in cost savings. If the organization closed too many locations or displaced too many employees, it could adversely affect the delivery of its core service and customer satisfaction. Also, quality could decrease. If customer service decreases enough, the market share and, ultimately, profit margins will decrease. Therefore, when analyzing performance and evaluating the overall vitality of an organization, it is very important to select appropriate metrics and understand the dynamics among them.

Aside from financial and operational performance, another key variable to review is stakeholder perceptions. Care should be exercised to review data from stakeholders across the entire value chain. This can include suppliers, shareholders, employees, customers, and competitors' customers. There are several studies that show an irrefutable relationship between selected stakeholder perceptions and organizational performance. Several other studies suggest a strong relationship between employee job/company satisfaction and customer satisfaction. A management team misses a large piece of the information puzzle if it does not understand the importance of key stakeholder perceptions.

Task 2: Determine Planning Horizon

A planning horizon projects how the organization will be planning its course. Most organizations have a planning cycle of between three and eight years. Obviously, as with most forecasts, the farther out you prognosticate, the greater the margin of error you will have.

Most managers do not spend enough time selecting the most appropriate planning horizon. Without much forethought, they then rush to produce a plan which is often outdated after the first year. This action often wastes labor and other resources, while still not providing for long-term success. Experience suggests there are five critical variables to consider when determining the planning horizon:

1. Volatility/predictability of the market
2. Product/service life cycles
3. Size of organization
4. Rate of technological innovation
5. Capital intensity of the industry

There is no hard and fast formula, but there are rules of thumb to follow. Generally speaking, there is a positive correlation between each of these variables and the length of the planning horizon.

The *more volatile* the external environment the *shorter* the planning horizon. This is because highly volatile and unpredictable environments have a greater forecasting margin of error. The *longer* the product/service life cycle, the *longer* the planning horizon. If your organization has very long product/service life cycles, then you have more time available to respond to changes in the market. The *larger* the size of the organization, the *longer* the planning horizon. This is because redirecting the efforts of many rather than a few employees requires considerably more time. The *faster* the rate of technological innovation, the *shorter* the planning horizon. If an organization operates in an environment where technological innovations are creating an order of magnitude changes (e.g., computers), planning cycles must be short to respond to ever-changing customer expectations. Finally, the *greater* the capital intensity of the industry, the *longer* the planning horizon. An excellent example is the utilities industry. The amount of money it takes in just bricks and mortar to produce power is measured in years. Just think about how long it takes to build a nuclear power plant.

Task 3: Conduct Environmental Scan

Environmental scanning is the process of assessing present and future conditions in the external environment that affect organizational performance. An environmental scan will identify and prioritize the opportunities and threats in the environment. This information is a critical input to developing vision and strategy.

Opportunity is defined as something happening outside the organization that enhances its ability to compete. Examples include deregulation, new technological innovation, or a competitor going bankrupt. Conversely, a threat is something happening outside of the organization that may limit its ability to compete. Examples include new government regulation, political instability in a country of operations, or rising energy costs.

Before conducting an environmental scan, it is important to identify all of the variables that can positively or negatively affect organizational performance. Exhibit 3.1 details some generic E-scan variables. These vary from company to company and must be identified before data collection begins. The most common questions asked are, "Where do I find all of this information?"

Experience suggests the data can be obtained from several internal and external sources. Depending on the size and sophistication of the organization, some sources may not be available. From an internal perspective, the first places to look are in the corporate strategic planning function, sales, and marketing departments. These units typically have a wealth of information on the industry, competitors, and trends/variables impacting performance. Many also have information on best practices and future trending. Additional internal sources include the corporate

Exhibit 3.1
Environmental Scanning Assessment Variables

Customers	Market	Competitors
• Strategic segmentation • Desired product/service attributes • Satisfaction levels • Key buying factors • Currency fluctuations	• Inflation rates • Interest rates • Energy costs • Unemployment rates • Currency fluctuations	• Product lines • New technology • Growth rate/trends • Operational/ financial results • Value chain analysis • Market segmentation
Government • New laws • Regulation • Deregulation • GNP	**Demographic** • Age distribution • Geographic shifts • Socio-economic trends • Changes in buyer values • Changes in lifestyle	**Industry** • Product life cycles • Buyer values • Key buyer groups • Industry sales • Access to raw materials

Stakeholder:
• Stockholders
• Unions
• Suppliers
• Customers
• Employees

library, the investor relations department, customer service, and quality functions.

Externally, there are many more resources to tap. These include the Internet, trade, industry, and professional organizations, trade magazines, and think-tanks. Annual reports, brokerage houses, and governmental sources (census data, IRS, tax records) can also provide substantial information about industries and specific organizations.

Although the purpose of strategic planning is not to create full color deliverables (a strategic planning binder that collects dust on the credenza), visualizing some of the key components of a strategic plan is helpful. Exhibit 3.2 is a market/competitor analysis matrix from a chemicals manufacturing business. This matrix is extremely useful to

Exhibit 3.2
An Example of a Competitor/Market Matrix

Key Market Segments	Competitors	Strategy	Sources of competitive advantage
Paper/textiles	Berol*	Increase market share	Outstanding sales force
	CIBA	?	
	Akzo	?	
	Stepan	Consolidation	?
Mining	Toma Products*		Low cost manufacturer
	FMC	Low cost manufacturer	?
	Akzo*	?	Strong senior management team
	James River	Diversification	?
Personal Care	Goldsmidt*	Product focused	World class time to market
	McIntrye*	?	Low debt, well capitalized
	Albright & Wilson*	Growth through acquisition	Leader in Eastern Europe
	Rhone Poulonc	?	?
Laundry Products	Stepan*	?	Backward vertically integrated
	Akzo*	Product focus	60% of revenues from new products
	Lanza	Customer focus	?
	Hoesch*	?	Strong brand equity
	Novartis	Divest non-strategic businesses	?

? = Missing or inadequate information

begin to understand why certain competitors have historical/current performance levels. Additionally, this data can help focus discussions on how to best attack competitors where they are most vulnerable.

The other environmental scanning variables can be categorized according to whether they are opportunities or threats. Several different formats have been tried, but a workshop format that includes senior management and key stakeholders works best. As you might expect, the key is to obtain consensus on the most critical opportunities and threats and not become bogged in onerous lists that include the "trivial many." Following are examples of the most strategic opportunities and threats that a manufacturer recently identified:

Opportunities:

- Competitor Ajax is in Chapter 11; several of its plants can be purchased at considerably below market rates
- Natural gas expenditures can be reduced by generating electricity through waste to energy
- Large untapped markets in Latin America and Russia
- Non union plants
- Make better use of global harmonization (share best practices, etc.)

Threats:

- AMPAX, one of our key customers, is being sold to Thermo Co., which buys its raw materials from our competitors
- Product price increases hard to justify and hold in a soft market
- Economic conditions in Asia directly impacting product demand
- Employees don't sense urgency to change
- New government environmental disposal regulations come on line next year; Alpha and Beta plants cannot cost effectively be brought into compliance
- Boston and Hartford plants are targeted for unionization

Task 4: Identify Key Success Factors (KSF)

A key success factor describes those things at which an organization must excel to be successful in the marketplace. KSF are identified as an outgrowth of the environmental scan and are important because they are a critical input in developing business strategy. Common examples of KSF are as follows:

- Strong technical support
- Reliability
- Small product lines
- Low cost provider
- Strong sales function
- Innovation
- State of the art technology

Key success factors are easily identified via the following three steps:

1. Identify the most successful industry competitors.
2. Compare the most successful companies to average and below average performers; determine specifically what separates those organizations that "walk on water" from those "treading water."
3. Determine what part of the value chain (e.g., R&D, Sales, Marketing) is most strategic for each of the industry leaders.

Task 5: Complete Gap Analysis

A new trend which may be a remnant of the quality management movement has developed: too much attention is given to events outside the organization, and not enough attention is directed internally. A good strategy requires merging external environmental data with a thorough understanding of an organization's *internal strengths and weaknesses*. A performance gap analysis is a technique that can be used to identify the strengths and more importantly the weaknesses of an organization. When completing a performance gap analysis, it is not unusual to generate a long list of performance gaps or weaknesses. Moreover, strategically prioritize these gaps to address the most critical ones when developing the business strategy. Exhibit 3.3 illustrates the gap analysis process.

Earlier in the book we introduced the concept of architecture. Regardless of business size, it is comprised of *technology* (the applications used, Information Systems platforms and hardware, and adequacy/sufficiency of data), *processes,* and *organization* (HR systems, culture, competencies, etc.) architectures. A performance gap analysis should focus on identifying gaps between the strategy and each element of architecture.

Data can be collected via interviews, a review of appropriate documentation, historical performance data, benchmarking, focus groups, and targeted surveys.

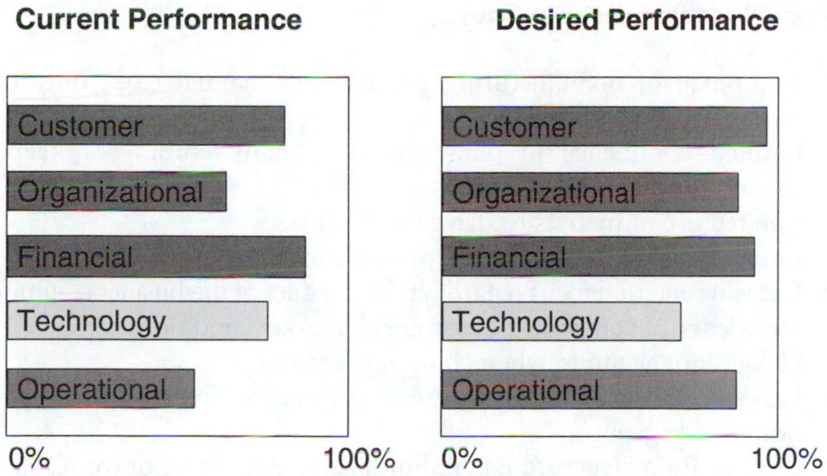

Current Performance

Desired Performance

Exhibit 3.3 *A Conceptual Overview of the Gap Analysis Process*

The following list of strengths and gaps help streamline analysis for a large manufacturing plant. Plant-wide strengths are noted along with plant-wide technology, organization, and process performance gaps. A gap analysis then should be completed for each function/unit within the scope of analysis.

Plant-Wide Strengths:

- Enterprise Resource Managing RP system up and running
- Several new products from other plants are successfully integrated
- Sulfonation reactor technology state of the art
- No safety accidents
- Employees are committed to success of the plant, have pride in their work
- Strong leadership team
- Operators willing to learn, accept responsibility and ownership for their decisions
- Good labor/management relations
- Strong responsiveness to customers
- Knowledgeable workforce with long tenure
- Willingness to change at high level

Plant-Wide Performance Gaps

- Too much of manufacturing process still manual (e.g., only one automated drum filler)
- Limited confidence in data integrity (many employees keep a shadow system)
- Limited use of metrics to drive the business
- Limited internal capability for non-technical training
- Excessive internal focus regarding the conduct of the business—limited knowledge of competitors, customers, market conditions
- Gauges not accurate when charging reactors
- Excessive internal focus—not enough people involved in associations, trade groups
- Organization structure has redundancies (Quality Control/Quality Assurance, three different people doing purchasing and logistics)
- Poor communications, especially across functions
- Doing vs. planning orientation
- No shared knowledge to incorporate learning
- Plant layout impedes plant performance: Kettle area A overbooked, Kettle area B underutilized; difficult to make A product in B kettles; easement runs through plant; piping restricts flexibility
- Lack of knowledge as to technology trends, best practices
- Decision support applications very weak
- More reactive to problems vs. prevention and planning
- Customer complaints too high and unresolved
- Speed of implementing change too slow with no accountability for deadlines
- HR systems (Performance mgt., rewards, recognition) not aligned with major objectives and initiatives
- Not enough plant personnel have ongoing direct contact with the customer

Task 6: Create Vision

To envision or not to envision? The strategic planning process can be an exercise in frustration, if time and effort is invested in areas that provide little value-added. A key decision point is to determine whether a vision statement is needed.

Let's start with a working definition of the word. A vision is a description of the desired end state of the business. It should create a picture in the mind of each reader that tell each one what the organization will be like in the future. A well-crafted vision will describe how the environment is different; elaborate on the prevailing values of management; be realistic; and evoke or compel others to achieve it.

If your organization is at a "crossroads," the company's vision statement can be used to create disharmony between the "as is" state and the "desired" state. The vision can serve to identify and elevate the pain or driver for the change. On a behavioral level, it can push stakeholders out of their comfort levels so they can be more open to change. This is what creates the momentum for change.

Be careful not to develop visions exclusively by the senior management team. Although this may be the logical starting place, the vision should be communicated to stakeholders throughout the organization and time should be spent in soliciting feedback so the vision can be made attractive to optimize stakeholder buy-in. The more effective management is at communicating the vision, the more motivated stakeholders will be in helping to realize it. After all, isn't that what senior management is all about: setting direction and managing expectations?

Task 7: Develop Business Strategy

The strategic focus is the central business theme that extends throughout the company. It is the guiding principle that differentiates one company from another in the market place. *It is the primary focus of the company.* The reasoning is simple and straightforward; a strategic focus:

- drives the way the company will market its product and services
- determines how the company allocates resources
- sets the context for everything from performance measures to corporate-wide initiatives

Creating a strategy is challenging because it requires the assimilation of all the data identified in the previous six steps. Specifically, the key inputs are corporate mandates, the key success factors, the most critical external opportunities and threats, the most strategic performance gaps, and organizational strengths.

Unfortunately, developing a strategy is much more of an art than a science. No formula is appropriate for every organization. When working with our clients, we generally follow these steps:

1. Determine the strategic focus of the organization. In Chapter 2, we discussed the three strategic focuses: being a cost leader, having a product focus, or having a customer focus
2. Create a strategy to either exploit organizational strengths and take advantage of opportunities in the market, or address weaknesses and respond to threats from competitors
3. Identify the assumptions underlying each strategy
4. Make sure the culture is aligned with the strategy

A well-designed strategy should also adhere to these guidelines:

- Strategies should not be in conflict with each other
- Lower level strategies should support higher level strategies (e.g. departmental strategies should support plant-wide/corporate strategies)
- Strategies must be consistent with internal policies, styles of management, philosophy/values, and operating procedures
- Resources and capital to see the strategy through to successful implementation must be sufficient.
- Risks must be identified and evaluated before pursuing a strategy

Once the strategy has been fully crafted, we strongly recommend you align the organization using the model depicted in Exhibit 3.4. For an explanation on how to use this model, refer to Chapter 1.

Task 8: Create Corporate Scorecard

At this point in the book, we provide a brief overview of the corporate scorecard. In Chapter 8 we will define in detail a working definition of the corporate scorecard; introduce guidelines for creating a scorecard; present scorecard templates; and discuss how the scorecard can be used to ensure organization alignment and execute the business strategy.

To understand the corporate scorecard concept, we suggest the reader think of the scorecard as the gauges on a car's dashboard. One must have constant readings relative to fuel consumption, alternator, oil pressure, and water temperature. Multiple gauges are also needed to determine the performance of an organization. A well-designed corporate scorecard should:

- Cascade from the business strategy
- Balance internal/external focus and quantitative/qualitative metrics

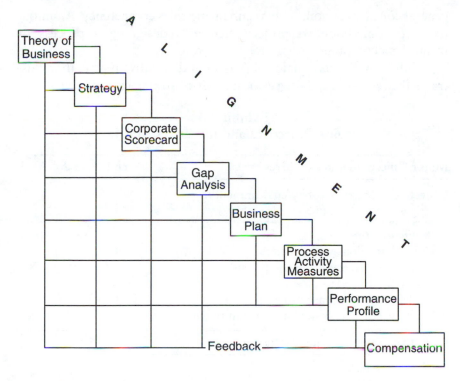

Exhibit 3.4 A Model for Aligning the Organization With Strategy

- Contain leading, trailing, and trending measures
- Focus on results and activities
- Not be overly complex or burdensome
- Change as needed over time to respond to environment

A critical point we make throughout this chapter is that *strategy is not static.* The focus is not to put this strategy in a nice binder and call it a strategic plan. *A strategy is a map.* Metrics should be used to regularly assess where the organization is relative to where management wants it to be.

Task 9: Identify Strategic Objectives and Initiatives

How will the organization implement its strategy? The difference between an objective and an initiative is subtle. An objective refers to a general course of action, such as enhancing sales competency. An initiative is a time-bounded project such as redesigning a process or installing a computer system.

Exhibit 3.5 depicts a major objectives and initiative matrix that illustrates the relationship between a number of strategies and tactics.

Exhibit 3.5
Major Objectives and Initiatives Matrix

Major Objectives and Initiatives	Yr 1	Yr 2	Yr 3
Objective 1: Improve safety/environmental performance			
Initiatives/tactics:			
• Create hazardous waste policy	X		
• Install in-line monitoring equipment		X	X
• Create fire brigade	X		
• Implement zero release program	X		
• Purchase ethylene oxide removal equipment			X
Objective 2: Improve quality/customer service			
Initiatives/tactics:			
• Implement SPC system	X		
• Implement housekeeping system		X	
• Provide problem-solving training to operators		X	
• Study layout of control room & lab and identify improvement opportunities	X		
Objective 3: Reduce operating costs			
Initiatives/tactics:			
• Implement cycle time reduction program		X	
• Outsource warehouse function	X		
• Outsource grounds maintenance department	X		
• Design and implement high performance work teams			X
Objective 4: Improve business and manufacturing processes			
Initiatives/tactics:			
• Develop and install a balanced scorecard	X		
• Link scorecard to management reporting, reward, and recognition systems		X	
• Purchase and install an ERP system		X	X

Major Objectives and Initiatives	Yr 1	Yr 2	Yr 3
Objective 5: Improve organizational capability			

Initiatives:

	Yr 1	Yr 2	Yr 3
• Create and execute individual development plans for all senior managers	X		
• Provide training to all operators on products, customers, understanding plant financial performance, and how their efforts affect plant performance		X	
• Provide management training and action learning experience for all members of senior plant management		X	X

Task 10: Execute Strategy

Most strategies are executed over a period of several years. Changes in the environment require ongoing review. The creation of contingency plans guard against the effects of unplanned events which negatively impact business. During the environmental scanning process, the key variables that impact organizational performance were identified. Those variables that are most likely to occur and have the largest impact on the business should be monitored regularly. Adverse impact to the business can be minimized by identifying specific triggers for the most critical variables and developing contingency plans to address these issues. For example if your business consumes a lot of oil, perhaps an excessive price increase will trigger a switch to co-generation.

The steps for developing contingency plans are:

1. Identify scenarios of what can go wrong
2. Assess probability of occurrence
3. Determine degree of adverse impact
4. Develop contingency plan

Once contingency plans are in place, create an evaluation strategy. This identifies how often the strategic plan will be reviewed; clarifies who is responsible for evaluations; specifies how data will be collected; identifies variances; analyzes causes; and determines the specific procedures for updating the plan.

Since the strategic plan is a tool to enhance management direction setting and decision making, it must be integrated with other related organizational systems. Exhibit 3.6 depicts the common interfaces with the strategic planning process.

The integration of strategic planning with the management reporting, rewards, and budgeting systems is particularly important. Most management reporting systems do not provide the right data, in the right format, at the right time, to the right person. The management reporting system should provide feedback to identify performance variances in sufficient time to take corrective actions. To a great extent, execution is dependent upon clearly communicating performance expectations and rewarding those behaviors and results that are aligned with the business strategy. Most organizations approach the budgeting process from an artificial perspective. Typically, each function/unit is provided an additional budget that is applied across the board, irrespective of the strategic importance of the unit. For example, in a pharmaceutical company the most important parts of the value chain are research and development, and sales. Doesn't it make sense that these functions receive more money than perhaps a staff function?

Summary

A strategy is the business road map to financial success. The strategy provides direction from where you are to where you want to be. An effective strategy must be a top down process. The process starts with the creation of an enterprise-wide strategic plan. From this plan, the Strategic Business Unit and functional strategic plans are created. The strategic planning process must be time bound, easy to understand, and

Exhibit 3.6 Strategic Planning Linkages

expedited through the use of standard tools. The following 10 tasks, regardless of whether you are in enterprise-wide, SBU, or functional strategic planning, will help the company's management team develop a strategy:

1. Conduct current situation analysis
2. Determine planning horizon
3. Conduct environmental scan
4. Identify key success factors
5. Complete gap analysis
6. Create vision
7. Develop business strategy
8. Create balanced scorecard
9. Identify tactics and initiatives
10. Execute strategy

Organizational Architecture

4

The concept of architecture was introduced in Chapter 2. Specifically, this chapter describes organizational architecture, explains its importance as a major component in achieving a company's business strategy, and presents a framework for achieving a competitive advantage.

What Is Organizational Architecture?

Organizational architecture is the human side of the company. It includes the skills and competencies a company needs to be successful, how communication will be accomplished with employees and the outside world, the control systems needed to ensure smooth company functioning, the performance measurement system to assess direction and success, the human resource system to manage people issues, structure to show people where they work and their relationship with other parts of the company, business systems to provide the productivity tools needed, and culture, the glue that binds the company together. It is composed of the following elements.

- **Communications**. This is responsible for getting company information to managers, employees, Wall Street analysts, and other stakeholders. Communications is often the only link a large number of employees have with management. This should be frequent, candid, and forthcoming about the state of the business. Communications shapes any major change effort.

- **Core Competencies**. These are the knowledge, skills, and abilities that reside in the workforce. Organizations that don't have a focused or formalized strategy frequently don't fully appreciate the link between core competency and company performance. Gaps between the core competencies and the focused strategy are a common problem in most companies today. Core competencies are composed of:
  - *Competitive Intelligence*. The skillful use of industry trends, key success factors, and benchmarking or other inter-company comparative data is competitive intelligence. Most companies have competitive intelligence on key processes such as customer service cycle times, market share, return on equity, etc.
  - *Technical Expertise*. This includes knowledge relative to computer applications, computer systems, data access/retrieval, or the specific technical skills. Pharmaceutical R&D, actuarial science, software design, and implementation are all industry specific expertise.
  - *Organizational Capability*. Leadership, organizational learning, and employee productivity comprise organizational capability. Leadership includes communicating, directing, negotiating, influencing, adapting, and gaining employee commitment. Organizational learning is the ability to learn from competitors, employees, and mistakes, without the threat of punishment. In many companies, organizational learning is a competitive advantage. Employees are more productive when they believe management has the skill to lead them to success and to provide them with the knowledge and resources they need to meet customer requirements. All of these attributes are interconnected, as depicted in Exhibit 4.1.

Exhibit 4.1

- **Administrative Control Systems.** Go to any *Fortune* 1,000 company in America, and you will typically find one or more binders on the "do's and don't's" that govern manager and employee behavior. These policies address a wide range of issues from diversity and sexual harassment to paid time off. In some companies where the culture is well-defined and strong, there is an additional set of unspoken rules that further define employee behavior. Culture will be treated more thoroughly later in the chapter.
- **Performance Measurement System.** The concept of a performance measurement system is relatively new to many companies, especially as a management tool. Traditionally, performance measurement was seen as a Human Resources activity. But the advent of the corporate (or balanced) scorecard has changed that. The corporate scorecard and its subordinate system, performance management, are considered some of the most powerful management tools of the late 1990s.
- **Corporate Scorecard.** This is a critical management tool used to prioritize efforts and focus accountabilities. The corporate scorecard is driven by the strategic focus, strategic goals, and the key performance measures that show the degree to which the strategic focus is being achieved. It is discussed in greater detail in Chapter 7.
- **Performance Management.** The performance management cycle includes performance planning, assessment, coaching, development, recognition, and compensation. You can find more about this topic in the chapter on individual and job performance measures.
- **Human Resource Systems and Policies.** The HR systems in no small way define employee behavior. Since filters are used to hire, promote, develop, reward, and punish (termination and progressive discipline), they have a profound impact on shaping employee behaviors. The level of sophistication and formality of these systems varies from company to company, but the key HR systems are the following:
  - *Recruiting.* This system identifies hiring specifications, creates a recruiting strategy, and initially screens candidates. Top companies have a formal recruiting strategy that ensures that the pipeline is filled with potential candidates. This includes newsprint ads and college recruiting programs. Potential candidate information is kept in relational databases, sorted by skills and location or other demographics, and shared over the company's Intranet, reducing recruiting costs.

- *Selection.* The ability to select the right employee for the right job is the best return on the investment that any company can make. Most managers are happy if they can hire a warm body that meets the minimal requirements of the job description. More sophisticated managers use tests, structured interviews, and role-playing. Their hit ratio, the percentage of top quality hires they make, is often four or five time higher than at those companies where such techniques are not employed.

- *Succession planning.* This system varies markedly from company to company. For many, this means identifying key positions, "ready now" and "future" successors, and "high potentials," and developmental planning for key management personnel and successors. Unfortunately, succession planning in most companies is based on "the old boys' network" rather than on ability. This is one human resource system that most companies can greatly improve, and for which the return on investment will greatly increase.

- *Employee development.* This system improves, or develops, employee skills. There are many forms of employee development from on-the-job training and classroom workshops, to coaching and mentoring programs. These programs can ameliorate skill and knowledge gaps relating to the companies' core competencies, their current job, or be used to prepare an employee for a new career opportunity.

- *Personnel systems.* Personnel systems include benefits and compensation administration, and payroll. Many of these subsystems are not strategy critical and can be outsourced.[1]

- *Employee relations.* Employee relations is a set of activities that is centered around employee satisfaction, organizational communications, and often union avoidance. Over the years, this set of activities evolved where the focus is now placed on employee non-work-related problems. Many Human Resource professionals believe their role is critical to corporate success, but often line management believes the HR professionals have become quasi social workers.

- *Organization structure.* This refers to the type of structural boundaries between units, staffing levels, and the way jobs are designed. Process-oriented companies are structured according to the key processes of each company. This occurs more often in manufacturing companies than others. Function-oriented companies are structured according to the various functions of finance, sales and marketing, human resources, manufacturing, etc. This is

by far the most common form of company structure. Geographic companies are based on their location in the country or the world. Some large consulting firms have a geographic structure, as well.
- *Strategic planning.* Once out of vogue but now back in full force, strategic planning is concerned with the long-term direction of the company. It typically has a two to five year planning horizon. See Chapter 3 for more information.
- *Annual business plan.* This is used to close gaps between targeted performance measures of the previous performance period's corporate scorecard and the actual results. Chapter 8 has more information.
- *Finance system.* This formal control mechanism accounts for money within the company. Companies are generally bound by the SEC, IRS, and FASTB regulations; nevertheless, there are many ways in which money is handled and accounted for within an organization.
- *Culture.* In this book, culture is defined as a system of prevalent beliefs, norms, values, and attitudes held by the vast majority of the employees within the company. In most companies there are multiple cultures at work at any given point in time. For example, a company may have a firm-wide culture that can be described as achievement-focused, teamwork oriented, and customer-focused. This culture may be very different in a specific locale or function. The culture of an office in the Deep South may be entirely different than the culture of an office on the West Coast.

Why Is Organizational Architecture So Important?

The organizational architecture is the personal interface between technology and process architectures. Organizational architecture drives employee behavior. Like it or not, most managers believe that employees always resist change. History is replete with companies whose management wanted to change their strategy but were unable to execute this change, because they did not understand the link between organizational architecture and employee behavior. *All major changes in strategies must be accompanied by changes in all the major components of the organizational architecture, especially the performance measurement system.*

The strongest change lever in organizational architecture is the performance measurement system. If behaviors need to be changed, considerable attention must be focused on how managers and employees are measured. Devising a performance measurement system that focuses as much attention on the activities performed as it does on results achieved greatly improves the chances that any large company-wide initiative will be a success. For additional information on individual and job performance measure, see Chapter 10.

Who Owns the People Organizational Architecture?

There is much discussion, sometimes bordering on conflict, about whom should "own" various aspects of the organizational architecture, particularly those parts of the architecture that deal directly with employees. The discussion has swung like a pendulum for the last 25 years. In the seventies and early eighties, line management had the primary ownership; since the late 1980s, the systems are now the responsibility of the Human Resources function in many companies. But, once again, the pendulum is swinging back, this time in favor of line management. Research suggests the shifting of responsibility is a direct result of several factors.

- The excesses of the early '80s led to over-population of manager and staff positions, greatly increasing overhead. During the reengineering era of the early 90s, manager and staff positions were cut dramatically. Some responsibilities for employees that managers had were transferred to the HR function, simply because management's span of control had increased so much. More responsibilities shifted to the HR function, also caused by state and federal rules and regulations, and the increasing number of lawsuits based on these new regulations.
- Many line managers began to think that the human resource function was only an employee advocacy function, interfering with their right to make business decisions on such things as head count, compensation, and hiring and firing. HR professionals were concerned about management's ability to make critical decisions which were in compliance with all the federal and state regulations. This conflict still exists, because many managers perceive that HR policies strangle

them with CYA bureaucracy while human resource professionals believe they save their company millions in legal judgments by running interference between employees and managers.

- The concept of Human Resources is a fairly recent one, since the mid-seventies. Before then, HR was called "personnel" and was primarily concerned with employee relations, benefits, and compensation. But the gradual change to a service economy created high labor costs, in some cases as high as 90%. When the capital allocation for labor and talent runs into the billions of dollars for a large company, that huge capital allocation needs to be strategy critical and better managed. Human Resources needs to be a strategic partner.

A Reengineered Human Resources

Ownership of the organizational architecture should be shared between line managers and Human Resources. HR is a staff function that supports the line functions to achieve the business strategy. HR also has an important view of how a company works and brings its own set of unique skills to identify gaps between the business strategy and the organization architecture.

Re-crafting responsibilities begin with the reengineering of the HR function. This helps alleviate some doubt in line managers' minds about HR managers' capability to address business issues. Reengineering Human Resources helps managers better understand where they should get the help they need to make employee decisions, or the tools and techniques they need to solve company and individual performance problems.

Not all HR professionals have the skills to be strategic partners with line management. Far too many are only concerned with the well-being of the employee and not with making money. Others are capable of learning new skills, but only a very few will have the opportunity to focus on making the company more effective and profitable. The value of the HR function is reflected in the products and services offered, and the impact it has on the company.

The new model (Exhibit 4.2) consists of four distinct quadrants. The quadrant arranged along a vertical axis defines added value to the company, and a horizontal axis defines change affecting the number of individuals affected at one time. Simply put, the larger the number of people involved, the greater the impact on the organization, largely in terms of costs, increased performance, or lost opportunity costs.

Exhibit 4.2
The Redesigned Human Resource Function for the Year 2000

	Low Impact	High Impact
High Value	**Staffing** • Recruiting • Selection • Training • Education • Succession planning	**Performance Consulting** • Organizational assessment • Change management • Performance improvement • Process improvement • Performance measurement • Strategy implementation
Low Value	**Benefits and Compensation Planning** • Benefits planning and administration • Compensation planning and administration	**Employee Service Center** • Payroll • Payroll paper work • Benefits Q&A • Compensation Q&A • Workers compensation • Short-term disability • Work Family programs

In this exhibit:

• Staffing is in-house recruiting, selection, training, education, and succession planning, and having employees prepare for work.
• Benefits and Compensation Planning creates its plans to support the strategy of the company.
• The Employee Call Center, generally found in large companies, is the one place an employee or manager must contact to make personnel changes, such as address and benefits changes. Many of these are accessible on the company intranet.[2]
• Performance Consulting is housed under Operations, Strategy, or Finance. In this model, Performance Consulting has the highest added-value and the greatest impact; Benefits and Compensation has the lowest value and the lowest impact. Many people will find this assignment of Benefits and Compensation to the low value-low impact quadrant mysterious. Research shows that neither function significantly increases nor maintains productivity over extended periods of time.[3]

- Performance Consulting provides middle and upper management with the tools and techniques they need to improve company and human performance. Performance consultants have the skills to lead company assessment, change management, performance improvement, process improvement, reengineering, and performance measurement projects.

Culture in Organizational Architecture

To most line executives, the word "culture" represents a vague notion. Most of the early studies in corporate culture adopted the basic anthropological definitions of culture, which included a description of prevalent beliefs, norms, values, symbols, attitudes, and unwritten rules held by the vast majority of the employees within the company (Exhibit 4.3). To many, this definition was just an entanglement of concepts that were too hard to operationalize.

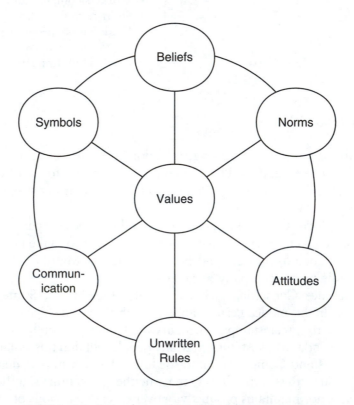

Exhibit 4.3 Conventional Model of Corporate Culture

Instead of insisting that company is driven by its culture, it is now understood that corporate culture is fashioned to support a company's strategy. Culture is driven by many aspects of the company, process, and technological architectures; therefore, it is an output of those architectures. But culture is also self-reinforcing and, therefore, an input for the architectures (Exhibit 4.4).

For the company to be successful, culture must be driven by the business strategy, not the other-way-around. The company's existing culture forms a "behavioral boundary" that affects the degree to which a strategy is implemented. Fortunately, culture, as well as behavior, can be changed over time. This is accomplished by identifying which employee behaviors need to be changed to achieve the business strategy, *not* which

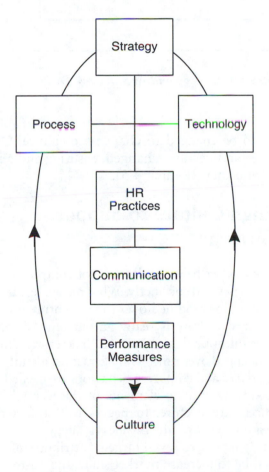

Exhibit 4.4 Culture as a Self-Reinforcing Behavior Change

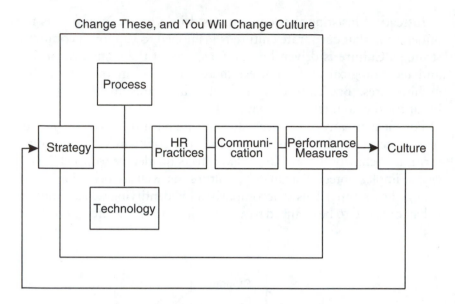

Exhibit 4.5 *Strategy and Architecture Driven Culture*

behaviors need to be changed to change the culture. Only then are pieces of the three architectures changed, ensuring and reinforcing the required behavior change (Exhibit 4.5).

How to Align Culture to Support Business Strategy

Unlike most others, we believe culture is both output and input. Every existing culture is described succinctly. What most executives don't realize is that culture can be modified over time to ensure it is aligned with the business strategy. Culture is really an outcome of the technology, process, and organizational architecture. Therefore, culture can be manipulated or changed over time. Managers must identify what type of cultural characteristics and employee behaviors are needed to realize the strategy. By modifying specific elements of the technology, organizational, and process architecture, managers will craft a model which ensures culture is aligned with the business strategy.

Start by identifying five to seven targeted attributes of your business strategy. It could be to increase market share and customer retention. Next, ask yourself what type of cultural characteristics and employee behaviors are needed to achieve this strategy. Identify five to ten clear attributes. Relative to desired cultural characteristics, this can include such things as low bureaucracy, high operational flexibility to respond quickly to market changes, and aggressive use of technology to enable the core processes. Desired employee behavior could include a willingness to learn new skills, becoming deft at developing and maintaining customer relationships, and demonstrating flexibility regarding job assignments. The desired cultural characteristics and employee behaviors will evolve over time if the technology, organization, and process architecture is modified. This includes:

- Using relational data bases to ensure information is available to lower level personnel for decentralized decision making
- Adopting imaging technology to enhance information availability
- Reducing the number of layers of management
- Implementing a skill based pay reward system
- Redesigning the physical layout to promote cross functional teamwork
- Reengineering the order entry process

Summary

In this chapter, we presented an approach for aligning organizational architecture to ensure it closely supports the business strategy. We made a case that alignment is the joint responsibility of both the Human Resources function and line management. HR managers must step away from their traditional areas of habit or comfort and learn new competencies. This will allow them to offer more value-added services. The line must clearly articulate their needs and provide a platform for a strategic partnership to exist with HR. The major components of organizational architecture are:

1. Communications
2. Core competencies
3. Competitive intelligence
4. Technical expertise
5. Organizational capability
6. Administrative control
7. The performance measurement system, including the corporate scorecard
8. Performance management
9. Human Resources systems and policies

10. Organizational structure
11. Business systems
12. Annual business plan
13. Financial system
14. Corporate culture

Endnotes

1. There are many outsourcing companies that are really quite good, such as Hewitt & Associates. But before any manager decides to outsource any of these systems, particularly payroll, he or she should conduct an exhaustive activity-based costing to ensure apple-to-apple comparison. Many managers fail to do this and find themselves being charged exorbitant fees that previously were nominal. For example, cutting a special bonus check can sometimes cost $200 or more from a vendor, this would have cost less than five dollars internally. If a company has thousands of exceptions, most managers would be better off keeping these subsystems within the company.

2. The Service Center and the administration of the benefits plan are very labor intensive but typically not a strategic activity. These activities can easily be outsourced and completed more economically by an outside firm. In some cases, this may be true of payroll as well, particularly if a company is small and has a simple compensation system. But organizations with more complex compensation plans have found that outsourcing payroll is not only a nuisance but expensive as well.

3. Despite popular belief, there has been no empirical research that shows whether benefits or compensation has any impact on productivity or company performance. Some evidence suggests that bonuses may actually be a performance disincentive for a larger number of people.

Technological Architecture

5

Introduction and Definitions

This chapter defines technological architecture and discusses some of the latest theories on managing alignment. Technological architecture includes:

- Information technology
- Telephony
- Operations and manufacturing technology
- Applications
- Desk-top technology
- The management of knowledge systems

Given the amount of space it would require to cover all of these topics, this chapter will focus primarily on the management information system, its relationship to the strategic focus, and how to build a strategy driven management information system.

The Conventional View of Technology Architecture

The conventional view of most management information system integrators is that information technology should drive strategy. While unwilling to often state this as an axiom, in practice it is reality. In a survey conducted by The Catalyst Consulting Group, with over 100 management information system integrators, less than 25% of the integrators believed business strategy drove the technology architecture.

Proponents of the conventional view of technology architecture believe it is broken into several sub-components. The components are listed and defined as follows:

1. **The Information Model.** The information model provides a map for managing the information flow:
   - Planning the resident location of data
   - How and where data is accessed within the organization
   - How data is attached to the workflow, documents, and personal files that span the company
   - The vital information objects or data categories (such as customer, transactions, location, date and time, product, money, and capital assets)
   - The interconnection between different business processes that own and maintain them
   - Database management and administration
   - The technology used to store, move and share information around the organization
   - Guidelines, performance standards and measures

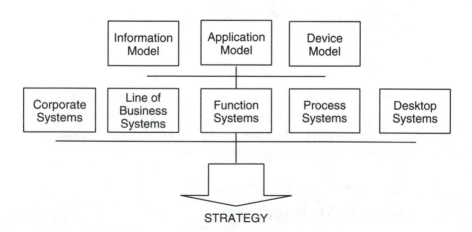

Exhibit 5.1 A Conventional View of Technology Architecture

- The use of transaction coordinators or monitors, structured query language (SQL), and relational or other types of database technologies

2. **The Application Model.** The purpose of the application model is to define the major kinds of applications needed to manage the data and support the business functions of the enterprise. This model describes the standard interfaces, services, and applications needed by the business. These translate into development resources for the project teams (e.g., component and code libraries, standards documents, design guidelines). The model describes the automated services that support the business processes and describes the interaction and interdependencies of the organization's applications. Also, it provides guidelines for developing new applications and moving to new application models. The application model also defines the applications needed to execute the business mission (i.e., topologies, development environments, APIs, security, network services, database management system services (DBMS), technical specifications, hardware tiers, operating systems, etc.).

3. **The Device Model.** This model defines the major kinds of equipment and devices needed to provide an environment for the applications managing the data. The device model includes:

   - Established standards and guidelines for the acquisition and deployment of client/workstation tools
   - Design/implementation application building blocks, infrastructure services, network connectivity components, and platforms

Some Problems with the Conventional View

Management information systems (MIS) are in their late adolescence. And like many teenagers, management information systems are full of contradictions, broken promises, and squandered youth. Its growth appears to be chaotic, uncontrolled, and unbounded. Its promises of youth have not been kept, causing senior management to be skeptical of claims of any reasonable returns on investments. As we speak, many managers are implementing enterprise-wide resource planning software, which may be the best or worst decision they make. MIS managers often drive new systems through the company, simply because it is their opinion that this is the right thing to do. In dozens of company surveys done by us, it is clear that very few CIOs can explain how their systems will help the strategic focus of the company. The costs are enormous.

- Each year $250 million are spent on management information system projects
- Less than 20% of the management information system projects are completed on time and on budget
- 30% of the projects are canceled before completed
- Costs average 190% of their original estimates
- Lost opportunity costs cannot be measured
- Less than 30% of the enterprise resource planning (ERP) projects are successful
- ERP projects have caused more than 20 companies to go bankrupt

The conventional view of the management information system (MIS) is that it lacks connection to the strategic focus. Some excruciating failures have resulted from this. Many organizations embarked on ERP as a solution to an ever-increasing need for information. Unfortunately, only a small percentage of these projects are successful. According to a 1999 survey by The Standish Group, an independent IT research company, the vast majority of these projects are completed over budget, late, and with too little realization of the theoretical benefits of the software. The reasons for project failure are similar to the reasons of reengineering failures in most companies. The root cause of these poor results are listed according to their rank importance:

- Little or no connection to the company strategy
- Incomplete requirements/specs and an overzealousness to implement all the modules, regardless of whether they were needed
- Not enough emphasis on organizational (i.e., people, business systems) issues
- Poor project management
- Lack of stakeholder commitment
- Ineffective training
- Lack of user input
- Processes not redesigned
- Unrealistic time frames
- Weak performance measurement

The Problem with Conventional MIS Performance Measures

Beyond labor cost, the cost for buying and maintaining the management information system is often the largest single expense in a company's budget, costing nearly 90% of total dollars spent. It is not uncommon for a single company to budget a billion or more dollars to buy and maintain the components of the MIS portion of the technological architecture.

Management wants clear, concise information on how well the stockholders' investments are used. This multi-million dollar layout for MIS causes many senior managers to question the economic utility of the MIS investment. Unfortunately, there is no consensus on which return-on-investment performance measures are valid. In *The Squander Computer*, Paul Strassman debunks all of the popular organizational-level performance measures used to evaluate management information system performance. There is no positive correlation between IS/technology capital allocations and revenue, return on equity, return on sales, return on shareholder value, economic-value-added (EVA), or any other financial measure.[1] In fact, there is generally an inverse relationship: the greater the IT expenditure, the less likely a company will be profitable. Large IT initiatives like ERP, are often capitalized at 5–6% of revenues. This means that such undertakings must have EVAs of 20% or more to cover the cost of money and make a profit.

This lack of valid organization-level MIS measures is in stark contrast to the control performance measures used to audit MIS. Here there is general agreement about what the MIS should and should not do.

Building a Strategy-Driven, Performance Measurement–Based MIS

An alternative to the conventional view of the MIS is a strategy-driven, performance measurement-based business view. This differs in that it puts business management, *not* MIS management, back in control of MIS. Equally important, the business view ensures that the strategic focus drives the MIS. The model proposed is loosely based on the work done by John Zackman, in the early eighties.[2] It was not widely adopted then, but his model is gaining currency today. See Exhibit 5.2.

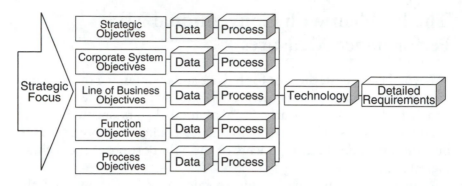

*Exhibit 5.2 The Business Objectives of the Management
Information System*

The business view of the MIS contains strategic, business processes, lines of business, functional, and process objectives. Each has its own data requirements, process requirements, technology (e.g., applications, equipment) and detail requirements. Once each of the views is defined, each view is further broken into data and process requirements. This high level view determines the *what* that should be automated, and determines how the data will be processed. The technology used and its detailed requirements should be left to IT experts. This approach eliminates artificial vertical boundaries between the end-users and the IT experts.

1. **The Strategic Objectives.** All IT applications, like all performance measures, should be driven by the strategic focus of the organization. Not doing so causes companies to invest in systems and equipment with poor return on investment (ROI) and in lost time and customers. The strategic focus should also drive the degree of centralization versus decentralization. Later in this chapter, a discussion of a strategic model of the MIS using a value chain from which strategic management information system goals and leading and lagging performance measures can be developed.

2. **The Corporate Objectives.** The corporate view of the MIS (which is equivalent to senior managers' objectives) is very different from the conventional view. The corporate view of the MIS is aimed at deriving as much information from the system as possible in order to ensure that senior management is:

- Maximizing value for shareholders and employees
- Effectively running the company
- Effectively countering the competition
- The implementation of Enterprise Resource Planning (ERP), balanced scorecard systems, activity-based management systems, database-driven human resource systems, and knowledge management systems are all current attempts at better managing the company.

3. **The Line of Business Objectives.** In this age of mergers and acquisitions, many companies have multiple lines of business. Each line has objectives that are cascaded from both the strategic and corporate objectives. But each line of business has its own information needs, such as:[3]

- Financial information
- Customer information
- Organizational information
- Operational information
- Research and development information

4. **Functional Objectives.** Functional objectives vary greatly across functional departments and may overlap with a line of business objectives. For example, each corporation has a human resource information system, but each line of business may have very different needs from that system: a different compensation program, or different staffing needs. Similarly, marketing and sales has very different systems requirements than manufacturing, legal and regulation departments. But all of these system requirements should be driven, not just by function needs, but by strategic MIS objectives.

5. **Process Objectives.** Processes typically traverse across multiple functions. For instance, a customer satisfaction data analysis process commonly touches sales and marketing. There can be considerable overlap between functional objectives and process objectives. But in general, process objectives are much more detailed and task oriented than functional objectives. Like all other objectives listed, process objectives should drive the MIS, not the other way around.

Given that most organizational-level financial performance measures lack statistical significance, are there other measures that are useful to

Exhibit 5.3
A Process-Driven View of MIS

Process Architecture

	Standards	Models	Processes	Inventory
Infrastructure				
Data				
Applications				
Functions				

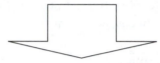

Technology Architecture

	Data	Functions	Networks	Roles	Time
Scope					
Enterprise Model					
Systems Model					
Technology Model					
Components Model					

management? The answer is Yes! A performance measurement system can be implemented as a means to ensure all aspects of the MIS are aligned with the strategic objectives. This can be accomplished via the following four steps:

1. Senior management and members from IT review the strategic focus of the company.
2. Senior management create a value chain based on balanced scorecard perspective that identifies a set of strategic objectives for the management information system.

3. Once the goals are established and agreed upon, management determines how these goals will be measured using outcome and contributing measures. See the example at the end of the chapter.
4. Management, along with the MIS team, agrees which initiatives will be attacked during the upcoming performance period.

In the past, senior management was inundated with pages upon pages of detailed computer printouts documenting primarily computer up-time, processing, transaction, and costs per personal computer. None of these so-called performance indicators helped senior managers manage the MIS. Many leaders, particularly senior management, are finding that having a balanced scorecard approach to management information performance measures greatly increases their ability to better manage the system, its costs, and feedback from customers and end-users.

MIS Change Management Questions

With this kind of investors' money at stake, more time and energy should be focused on asking a few simple questions and demanding some straightforward answers. The most important questions to ask about MIS are:

1. *How will this new MIS help the company achieve its strategy?* The strategic focus should be at the top of every manager's list when it comes to making IT decisions. But this question is seldom asked. Instead, management-by-magazine sometimes eliminates the discussion entirely, often leading to the results listed above.[4] It makes great strategic sense for Wal-Mart to have an

Technology & Innovation	Organization Perspective	Financial Perspective	Operational Perspective	Customer Perspective
Self Service				
Data Warehousing				
Archiving				
Data Mining				

Exhibit 5.4 A Balanced Scorecard Value Chain

ERP system. Wal-Mart is concerned with moving millions of items manufactured by thousands of companies. The greater the information need, the more automation can be brought to bear on large undertakings; and the more operational and strategic sense it makes. An ERP system **does not** makes much sense for Nordstrom. This company offers 10% of the products that Wal-Mart offers, and it has five percent of the vendors. But Nordstrom has the best customer-focused database in the industry, because its strategic focus is servicing its customers.

2. *What processes are needed to ensure that the MIS is designed to support the strategic focus, not the other way around?* In the rush to have the latest technologically advanced systems, many companies let their MIS drive their strategy. This is a decision that leads to years of shrinking margins and lost profits. If management decides that it has to change strategies and can justify a new MIS, then so be it. But such a company must have enough capital to ensure a healthy transition period. This additional capitalization may require as much as twice the current IT capitalization. Not many companies can afford such an expenditure.

3. *To what degree does the MIS aid in aligning the process and organizational architecture?* The most often cited reason for installing a new system is to increase productivity. However, many companies' managers who have installed the latest "whizbang" personnel system have found that in order to maintain frequent and expensive updates, they must run a "plain-vanilla" system. The downside of this uncustomized approach means there is often a dramatic increase in the number of manual work-arounds. Many managers find they have to increase human resource systems headcount just to make payroll in a plain-vanilla system. Similarly, many managers who switched to all the modules of an ERP system find their ability to meet internal and external deadlines greatly diminished.

4. *Can new products and services be introduced with a minimum of effort?* Management needs to assess the degree to which a new system is adaptable, flexible, and costly. What are the costs of adding new products or features to an existing line of business? What are the potential consequences of customizing the software? If Version 1.1 is customized, what consequences will that have on installing Version 2.0? What is the cost of migrating data from one version to another? What are user group members saying about their experience with adaptability and customization?

5. *To what degree does the strategic focus drive centralization or decentralization?* Generally, organizations that focus on operational excellence centralize their IT capabilities to reduce IT expenditures. Customer- or product-focused companies may be able to create a strong enough business case to carry the extra costs of decentralization as a by-product of better data to support operational decision-making.

Three-Phase MIS Project Guidelines

The core competency of technology vendors and systems integrators must be technology. Our experience suggests that implementing a new system affects a large number *of other aspects* of the organization, as well. All aspects of a company must be aligned to support the overall success of the systems solution. A well-conceived, large-scale systems project should include at least the following three phases.

Phase 1: Scoping and Risk Assessment

This begins with the creation of a cross-functional project structure which includes end users. The steering team usually creates a visual, detailed workplan, and performance measures to be used in focusing efforts and in evaluating the effectiveness of the solution. One of the initial tasks undertaken is a review of the strategic focus to ensure that the new application supports the strategy, not the other way around. This is followed by an organizational risk assessment. Data for this assessment is collected using a variety of methods including document reviews, interviews, focus groups, and short targeted surveys to:

- Finalize the technical requirements
- Identify sources/causes of resistance
- Understand the workforce characteristics and skill gaps
- Identify the specific impact the new system will have on the culture, non-technical competencies, job design, human resource practices, non-automated processes, organization design, and administrative policies.
- Quantify the impact on such systems and conduct an implementation risk assessment.

There are three non-technical deliverables completed at the end of this phase:

1. A detailed work plan with a scoping document covering all aspects of the organizational, process, and technological architectures; *and* change management
2. A communication and commitment strategy with targeted messages to management, implementers, users, employees, and vendors
3. A risk analysis detailing key risks and work around options

Phase 2: Solution Design and Implementation

Cycle times are dramatically reduced during this phase by employing "architecture labs." In most systems projects, different teams work on the technology, organizational, and process issues separately. Architecture labs utilize teams that work on the technology, organizational, and process issues simultaneously, thereby reducing cycle times and realizing more of the promised benefits of the system.

A common mistake made is the assumption that the project is completed once "you go live" with the new system. For those that have lived through this experience, you know how far from reality this is. Listed below are critical organizational management and process redesign issues that must be addressed during this phase:

1. Ensure the system aligns with the strategy and culture, not the other way around
2. Align critical non-automated business processes; these processes must be identified, prioritized, and selectively optimized so they do not become a bottleneck
3. Deliver a curriculum of targeted training to address identified skill gaps
4. Coach senior management to hold middle-management accountable and resolve people issues
5. Modify the organization structure, job designs, physical layout of work areas
6. Modify affected Human Resource systems such as the performance management system, compensation, and succession plans

Phase 3: Roll-out and Integration

During this phase it is critical to:

1. Analyze and fix any bottlenecks
2. Simplify or eliminate any workarounds
3. Ascertain which modules can be eliminated or added

Exhibit 5.5
An Example of Strategic Goals and Outcome and Contributing Measures for a Management Information System

Financial Perspective	Outcome Measures	Contributing Measures
• Support financial direction of CEO	• Reduction of technology expenses from imaging and other technological functionality	
• Find the most cost effective way of conducting business, not the cheapest • Identify all cross-functional impacts • Seek self-funding opportunities	• Ensure positive CBA	

Technology & Innovation Perspective	Outcome Measures	Contributing Measures

• Establish strategic criteria for selecting projects that fit tactically with HRIS strategic direction
• Ensure that existing and future technology can be highly scalable and leveraged such as:
  – Implement more modules of existing software
  – Cross functional/linkage and experience (e.g. data warehousing)
  – Simple user-friendly from the end user perspectives
	• Reduction of overall number of employee interactions	• Eliminate stand alone systems where possible
		• Eliminate manual workarounds
		• On time delivery of LOB balanced scorecard reports

(continued)

Exhibit 5.5 *(continues)*
An Example of Strategic Goals and Outcome and Contributing Measures for a Management Information System

Technology & Innovation Perspective	Outcome Measures	Contributing Measures
• Implement and maintain a "vanilla" strategy to meet business need • Provide the best technology based on business need, functionality, experience, support, future adaptability and costs • Consistent with AIM strategy	• Reduced maintenance costs • Vendors meet cost agreements • Vendors meet service level agreements • Depth of communication penetration with user groups • Number of technology rollouts to the lines of business	• Number of information sharing opportunities taken advantage of • Attendance at user group conferences • Increase in the number of audit and control consistency
• Exploit existing technology to expand user base or increase productivity and reduce exposure • Explain imaging functionality to other corporate areas		• % of work that is imaging-driven

Organizational Perspective	Outcome Measures	Contributing Measures

• Establish a working partnership with:
  – HRSC
  – 401k
  – Benefits Administration
  – Benefits Finance
  – Health & Safety
  – Compliance
  – Disability
  – Staffing
	• 100% customer satisfaction with service provided	• % of partners that receive technology and process training

Exhibit 5.5 *(continues)*
An Example of Strategic Goals and Outcome and Contributing Measures for a Management Information System

Organizational Perspective	Outcome Measures	Contributing Measures
• Develop specific decision-making group • The right people with the right skills in the right place, at the right time, with the right number of bodies • New competencies • Communicate extent and impact • Invest in developing IT people through training		

Customer Perspective	Outcome Measures	Contributing Measures
• Develop a strategy-driven customer model of how HRIS will interact with and service customers	• Establish one point of contact • 100% follow-up to all production crisis problems	• % of service level agreements established • % of service level agreements met
• Develop partnership with customers to: – Develop simple, utilitarian, user friendly processes – Focus on ease of use in redesigning processes – Focus on speedy access – Complete requirement of the MAP process	• 100% customer satisfaction with service provided	

(continued)

Exhibit 5.5 *(continues)*
An Example of Strategic Goals and Outcome and Contributing Measures for a Management Information System

Operational Perspective	Outcome Measures	Contributing Measures
• Achieve operational excellence	• Improve process throughputs (costs, cycle time, conformance to standards, quality, and quantity) wherever possible	• Improved cycle time on report requests
		• Improved change control process
		• Improved vendor management
		• Shortened acceptance test discovery time
		• Improved project management skills
		• Increased strategic awareness of:
		– Self service
		– Archiving
		– Data warehousing
		– Data mining
		– Build better tools

Summary

Management information systems (MIS) are costly for many reasons:

• The cost-benefit of new systems is nearly impossible to calculate with any degree of accuracy, but it must be done
• There is no satisfactory set of performance measures with which to judge performance
• The failure rate is much too high, sometime approaching 70% or more
• Its growth appears to be chaotic, uncontrolled, and unbounded

- MIS managers often drive new systems through the company, simply because it is their opinion that this is the right thing to do.

In order to contribute to a company's bottom line, managers must develop and implement an IT change model. It will then:

a. Include strategic, corporate, and line-of business-objectives for all of IT
b. Conduct an implementation IT risk analysis for any new corporate-wide implementation
c. Conduct cost-benefit analysis for any managers requesting IT changes
d. Develop standard, easily-modified reports
e. Hold all managers accountable for using the change model for any new IT changes

Endnotes

1. Strassman, Paul A. *The Business Value of Computers,* Introduction, pp. xvii–xix. New Canaan, CT: The Information Economics Press, 1990.
2. Zachman, John A. "A Framework for Management Information Systems Architecture." *IBY System Journal 26,* Number 3, 1987.
3. See Chapter 7, The Corporate (or Balanced) Scorecard, for complete definitions of these perspectives.
4. Management-by-magazine is one of the major management problems of the late 20th and early 21st century. Management at all levels assumes that because there was an article in a reputable magazine or journal praising the virtues of one solution to one customer, then this must be the solution for every company. Management-by-magazine has a large component of "me-too"-ism: If Joe Smith is implementing Whizbang ERP 1.0, then I must have Whizbang ERP 2.0.

Process
Architecture

6

What Is the Process Architecture and Why Is It Important?

Process architecture is the value chain of an organization, its collective processes, and the physical layout of offices and production facilities. Of all of the elements of architecture, the process element is the most important. If configured appropriately, the process architecture determines how an organization delivers its core product or service. The process architecture is designed to drive the technology and organizational elements of architecture.

Companies must be careful to avoid a "tail wagging the dog" situation. This occurs when technology drives the business in lieu of the process architecture driving the business. Take a step back and consider the irrationality of this situation. Would you base the purchase of a car for your personal use on whether it has a global positioning system in the dashboard? Most people would not! Logic would also dictate that organizations should first identify which part of the business is most strategic; streamline the underlying processes; and then build the organizational and technology architectures that enable these core processes. See Chapter 5 for more detail about the role IT should play in a company.

The Value Chain

"Value chain" is a term originated by McKinsey & Company and later enhanced by Michael Porter of MIT. The value chain is a graphic depiction of the activities an organization completes in designing, delivering, marketing, and supporting its core product/service. The value chain can be used to:

- Understand how an organization operates and what activities add the most value
- Identify the costs of key activities
- Compare organizations to identify sources of differentiation

Organizations don't operate in a vacuum. As a tool, the value chain provides an understanding of an organization's level of competitiveness, if it also includes the entire business interrelationships from suppliers through to the ultimate customer. See Exhibit 6.1.

Competitive advantage is, in part, a function of how well an organization is aligned with its suppliers, channel partners, and its customers. Successful companies tend to have key supplier processes aligned throughout the value chain. A good example of this is interfacing a supplier's order entry process with the company's procurement function. The suppliers' outputs (raw materials, sub-assemblies, information, etc.) become the input used in delivering the core product/service. Some organizations use a channel partner to sell and distribute to the ultimate customer. If an organization's key processes (e.g., operations, logistics) haven't been tightly aligned to the channel partner, then the relationship with the customer suffers. And lastly, if the channel partner's delivery capability is not in tune with the customer's requirements, sales revenues will suffer.

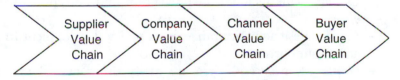

Exhibit 6.1 The Value Chain Linkages

Constructing a Value Chain

Value chains are composed of primary and support activities. Each type of a*ctivity* is further divided into several different *processes*. See Exhibit 6.2. Therefore, the exact configuration of a value chain will vary from company to company. The categories are defined according to their activities:

1. **Primary Activities.** These activities are directly involved in the creation/delivery of the core product/service, its sale, transfer to the customer, and after sales support. Primary activities can be further subdivided into:
   - *Inbound Logistics.* This includes all of the activities needed to provide inputs for the product/service.
   - *Operations.* This includes the activities that directly transform inputs into outputs.
   - *Outbound Logistics.* As its name implies, these are all of the activities used in getting the product/service to the channel partner or customer.
   - *Marketing & Sales.* Typically, this includes a wide range of processes that address product and market positioning through lead generation and sales.
   - *Service.* There are myriad service related processes an organization can use. This can range from equipment set-up and trouble shooting to product upgrade.

2. **Support Activities:** These activities are generally needed to ensure the primary activities are carried out:
   - *General Management.* The key elements of executive management address direction setting, focusing of employee efforts, coaching, and performance management.
   - *Quality.* This includes all prevention and detection focused efforts.
   - *Legal.* These activities range from policy development to litigation support.
   - *Human Resources.* There are many different HR systems/processes that drive employee behavior.
   - *Technology.* Technology incorporates a host of activities from policy and procedure development to office automation and R&D.

- *Procurement.* More commonly known as purchasing, this incorporates all of the activities that are responsible for bringing in raw materials and consumable supplies.
- *Finance.* This includes all of the accounting, treasury, policy-making and management-reporting activities.

The primary and support activities can be further subdivided into a number of processes. Exhibits 6.2 and 6.3 list examples of processes for each part of the value chain. The specific processes will vary markedly, based on the type of industry and sophistication of the business.

Exhibit 6.2
Example of Primary Processes

Logistics	Operations	Marketing & Sales	Research & Development	Service
Picking	Assembly	Market research	Applied research	Product installation
Packing	Fabrication	Advertising	Basic research	Warranty repair
Shipping	Equipment maintenance	Sales calls	Pilots	Customer training
	Production scheduling	Order processing		Troubleshooting problems

Exhibit 6.3
Example of Support Processes

Quality	Finance	Human Resources	Procurement	Technology
Raw material inspection	Closing	Succession planning	Expediting	Preventive maintenance
In-process inspection	Accounts payable	Compensation	Supplier selection	Design
Final inspection	Accounts receivable	Training & development	Invoicing	Development
Quality administration	Ledger	Performance management	Contract administration	Implementation
		Recruiting	Supplier certification	Stability program

Listed here are the steps for creating a value chain:

1. Developing a value chain is an iterative process. It begins with the development of a relationship map that at a high level depicts the key process or functional interdependencies. See Exhibit 6.4. The relationship map is useful in identifying the entire set of primary and support activities for each area in the business. This data is identified by reviewing existing archival documents, interviews, and focus groups. It is very important to understand when each activity starts; when it ends; how the underlying processes are completed; and how material and information flows throughout the organization.

2. Once the value chain for the organization is finalized, create a value chain that extends backward to suppliers and forward to channel partners and the ultimate buyer. Additional learnings take place if a value chain is constructed for key competitors.

3. Analyze the data to identify strengths, weaknesses, opportunities, and threats. The data is also insightful in determining the strategic focus of the company: a low-cost producer, product-focused or customer-focused. If there is some question about the degree to which processes align with the strategic focus, time should be taken to understand the impact this misalignment has on either the focus or the process.

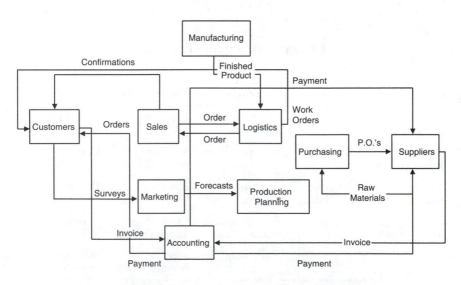

Exhibit 6.4 Example of a Relationship Map

Once the value chain is complete, answer the following questions:

- What parts of the value chain is each competitor trying to optimize?
- What parts of your value chain are not well connected?
- Are there any untapped opportunities for differentiation?
- Are there any significant cost differences between competing organizations, and are these potential sources of competitive advantage?

Physical Layout Analysis

The process architecture is closely interdependent with the physical layout of work areas. There is a strong correlation between work process efficiency and the layout of the physical area where work is being done. In its simplest terms, the greater the distances traveled, the longer the cycle times and the higher the cost of the activity both in hard and soft terms. From a behavioral standpoint, it's also a lot more difficult to promote teamwork if people are not physically co-located.

Physical layout analysis is a tool that can be used to:

- Identify how easily employees can access the facilities, equipment, and tools they need to compete their work
- Highlight physical barriers (bottlenecks and congested areas) that impede process efficiency and effectiveness
- Delineate structural or spatial limitations
- Identify the distance traveled from the beginning to the end of the process

The primary objective of physical layout analysis is to reduce unnecessary motion, reduce costs, and better utilize resources (equipment, facilities, tools, etc.). Research and experience in working with many clients suggests that a well designed physical layout has the following characteristics:

1. Work processes and physical layout are designed for joint optimization.

2. Office layouts and individual workstations are designed to minimize space requirements. All needed resources are located within easy access to employees.

3. Housekeeping procedures based on one of the most sacred Japanese management principles called "the Five S's," must be in place and strictly followed.

   a. *"Seiri"* means orderly arrangement. The Japanese believe that everything that is not absolutely necessary for completing the work at hand should be taken away and stored elsewhere.

   b. *"Seiton"* means orderliness. This translates to identifying the quantity and exact position of all needed resources. Although this may seem obvious, think about how much time is spent on a daily basis in most companies looking for resources to complete a job.

   c. *"Seiketsu"* refers to cleanliness. If everything has a predetermined location, then it is very easy to manage by exception. This eliminates the need for sophisticated and costly management control systems, because a simple glance is all that is needed to determine what is right or wrong.

   d. *"Seiso"* means constancy. People are creatures of habit. Standardization will shape employee habits and ensure variation is not introduced into the process.

   e. *"Shitsuke"* means discipline. The best plans and systems are useless unless people exercise the necessary discipline to follow the housekeeping principles.

Analyzing the Physical Layout

Since work is completed through various processes, physical layout is studied by tracing the flow of work from start to finish as it traverses the work environment. The primary output of layout analysis is a layout diagram. Layout diagrams are created at different levels of detail. A diagram can depict an overall process, a specific work unit, or even a specific work station. See Exhibit 6.5.

To many, this may seem like a very trivial activity; but let us pose one question: "Do you know how much physical distance is traveled in delivering your organization's core product or service?" We recently worked with a large, privately held, multi-national, publishing company that marketed a variety of reference books. Their process started with an idea (either an author contacted them with an idea or the publishing company identified an unmet need through market research) and ended with the manufacture of thousands of books. Since the organization was located in a large metropolitan city, it had office space in two nearby office towers. A layout analysis of the overall process revealed the process was primarily manual (moving bundles of paper) and traversed 29 floors between both buildings, involved over 50 people, and consumed more than 5,000 ft.

If you are thinking this is an anomaly, think again. The rudiments of physical layout are based in the concepts of just-in-time (JIT). Considerable cost and time can be removed from most processes by redesigning the physical layout to minimize space and travel distances. The use of JIT and advanced manufacturing techniques are two of the key reasons why the U.S. manufacturing industry rebounded so dramatically in recent years.

Steps in Constructing a Layout Diagram

We recommend managers take four steps to construct a layout diagram.

1. Review existing documentation. Most organizations have blueprints that depict utility locations, offices, stairwell, corridors, etc. It is integral for the non-engineer to work with a subject matter expert to become familiar with this technical information.

2. Document existing layout. Either document the core processes, or if available, use existing process documentation and superimpose this on the blueprints. Note travel distances, resources needed, congestion, and environmental constraints. Share the various iterations of layout diagrams with appropriate stakeholders to ensure the accuracy of the diagram and to maximize their buy-in.

3. Strategically prioritize layout problems. Develop a system for identifying problems. Then prioritize the problems using an A, B, or C method. "A" problems are the most strategic either because they have negative ripple effects throughout the organization or because they significantly impact the final product/service. "B" problems impede process efficiency but do not significantly affect product/service delivery. "C" problems are irritants and do not have considerable impact on product/service delivery.

4. Identify opportunities for improvement. We list some key questions that may be useful in analyzing physical layout:
   - Does the existing physical layout facilitate the type and amount of human interactions to optimally complete the work?

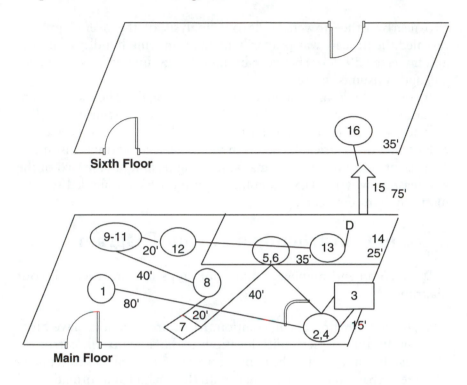

Exhibit 6.5 Example of a Layout Diagram of an Overall Process

- Does the layout provide easy access to required resources?
- Are the existing environmental conditions (noise, light, heat, etc.) conducive to the type of work being performed?

How Do I Align the Process Architecture?

The first key decision is determining which strategic focus area is most appropriate for the organization. As we indicated in Chapter 1, organizations don't have the resources, management capability, and core competency to simultaneously be "world class" from an operational, product, and customer perspective.

Low cost-focused companies provide customers with reliable products and services at the lowest cost delivered with minimal difficulty or inconvenience. Product-focused companies provide highly innovative products, while customer-focused companies provide a total solution to their customers. See Exhibit 6.6.

Exhibit 6.6
Key Characteristics of the Three Strategic Focuses

	Most Strategic Processes	Sources of Differentiation	Tactics
Low-Cost Focus	• Operations • Tightly link product supply, customer service, and demand management • Quality	• Quality • Price • Ease of purchase • Dependability • Transaction efficiency	• Standardized processes • Low overhead • Use technology as an enabler • No frills products/services • Centralized decision making
Customer Focus	• Customer service • Market research • Product/service delivery	• Customer relationships • Flexible products/services • Employee empowerment • Customer-driven performance metrics	• Utilize highly trained sales and service force • Decentralization • Strong customer data base • Create learning organization • Understand customers requirements
Product Focus	• New product development • Sales • Marketing • Recruiting	• Leading edge products/services • Best practices & future trending • Focus on solving problems	• Cross functional teamwork • Low bureaucracy • Educate customer • "Stretch goals" • Nontraditional structures

Once the strategic focus area is finalized, it is critical to identify which processes are most strategic for the organization. If your organization is focused on being the low-cost producer, employees must focus on the processes that deliver the core products/services and the key quality detection/correction processes. Customer focused organizations must optimize customer service, market research, and product/service delivery. Product focused organizations must optimize the new product development, marketing, and sales processes. Recruiting is also a key process because it takes the best minds to be the most innovative.

What does "optimize" mean? This is strategically allocating resources (budget, people, etc.). The most strategic parts of the value chain are allocated a greater proportion of resources. Let's take the non-generic drug pharmaceutical industry as an example. The most strategic parts of its value chain are R&D and Sales. And the most important processes within R&D and Sales are typically discovery, development, and advertising and promotion. The battle to achieve competitive advantage is won by optimizing these specific parts of the value chain. It's not typically won by being a world class manufacturer.

This sounds like "motherhood and apple pie," but just think how a budget is usually allocated. Experience strongly suggests the budgeting process is seldom well connected to the strategic planning process. At the beginning of each budget period, budgets are commonly increased by a specified percentage, regardless of strategic importance. Resources are considered, and they include the talent level of the people. If the organization is product-focused perhaps the senior management team may decide to pay at the 120% level for employees who work in the R&D function and only at the 85% level for individuals who work in finance.

The final component of aligning the process architecture includes a review, and if necessary, modification of the physical layout around the core parts of the value chain. This targets such things as the use of white collar cells to promote teamwork and a process orientation; co-location of interdependent personnel to facilitate response to market; the redesign of office layouts to reduce costs; or the elimination of IT functions that no longer add value.

Summary

Process architecture is without a doubt the most important of the three elements of corporate architecture when implementing the strategic focus. It is the engine that drives business. Competitive advantage is achieved by determining which parts of the value chain are most strategic, either differentiating these parts or optimizing how these parts are executed. The major component of the process architecture are:

The value chain, which is composed of

- Primary activities that are directly involved in the creation and delivery of core products and service

- Support activities that are in support of the primary activities
- The steps in developing a value chain are:
  1. Create a relationship map
  2. Review primary and support activities
  3. Create a preliminary value chain, going forward to the customer and backward to suppliers
- To construct a layout diagram, one must:
  1. Review existing documentation
  2. Document existing layout
  3. Strategically prioritize layout problems
  4. Identify opportunities for improvement

The Corporate (or Balanced) Scorecard

7

The corporate scorecard (or balanced scorecard) measures the achievement of the business strategy, communicates strategic direction, establishes key performance measures and performance targets at the organizational level. This is done by developing a performance measurement system with multiple perspectives (i.e., categories, such as financial, customer, organization, etc.), where for each perspective one to five key performance measures are developed.[1]

A working corporate scorecard can be a maze of interlocking business issues, systems concerns, senior management egos, and statistical complexity. Development and implementation of the corporate scorecard cannot be fully addressed in one chapter, maybe not even in one book. But this chapter will provide a solid overview of the corporate scorecard.

Why Corporate Scorecards Now?

Corporate scorecards, the term used interchangeably with the balanced scorecard, are relative newcomers to the world of business. The scorecard concept first appeared as the "family of measures" advocated by the statistical process control gurus and was later revised in Europe as the dashboard or the *tableau d'bord* by the socio-technical advocates. More recently the corporate scorecard was popularized by David Norton and Robert Kaplan in their articles and books.

Corporate scorecards evolved when it became apparent that traditional financial performance measures and the balance sheet could not help business leaders manage their companies in real time. Further, institutional investors are asking more and more of their portfolio companies to implement corporate scorecards.[2] The reasons are that traditional measures:

- Only provide a historic perspective, not a current perspective
- Focus too much managerial attention on the return on capital assets, especially when economic value added (EVA) is one of the KPMs[3]
- Distract management from sustaining and growing the business, which is often capital-intensive
- Disregard the business drivers that made financial success or failure possible
- Only look at the balance sheet which isn't comprehensive enough to manage a company
- Do not address the growing abundance of business data which needs to be focused on a limited set of business drivers to be understandable

These large investors are often mutual fund or large asset managers, or represent a company or organization's pension or 401K fund. To reduce their risks, these investors are asking their portfolio companies to develop and implement corporate scorecards. Their reasoning is they want a better understanding of what the management team thinks is important, and they want to know how well things are going. This requires a reliable and current performance measurement system.

Simply put, there are lots of activities being performed that ultimately lead to financial results, and these are not captured or controlled in financial reporting. Customer satisfaction produces financial results. This drives productivity, growth, and organizational learning. Jack Welch, well known for leading GE to success, says he only needs to know customer satisfaction, employee satisfaction, and cash flow to know how well his company is working at any given time.

Many companies have demonstrated mathematically the relationship between employee satisfaction, customer satisfaction, and financial success. Other companies have built dynamic computer simulations based on the scorecard, which has been remarkably accurate in predicting company success.

Scorecard Perspectives

Corporate scorecards come in a wide variety of configurations and are based on any number of systematic approaches to examining and measuring organizational-level performance. All corporate scorecards

Exhibit 7.1 The Relationship Between Financial Success and
Other Perspectives

have three to seven perspectives (read: "categories"). Different perspectives provide different ways of looking at the performance of a company through different eyes. Each perspective has one or more key performance measures. For example, the customer satisfaction perspective may have acquisition, retention, empathy, responsiveness, and business knowledge as key performance measures. Exhibit 7.2 addresses the approaches to examining the company performance.

For over 10 years, some companies have used the Baldrige Award Criteria as the foundation of their corporate scorecards. The seven perspectives from the Baldrige Awards are:

1. Customer satisfaction
2. Employee satisfaction
3. Financial performance
4. Operational performance
5. Product/service quality
6. Supplier performance
7. Safety/environmental/public responsibility

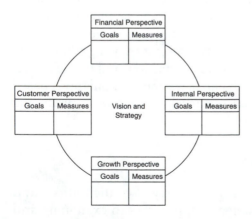

The Kaplan and Norton system has four perspectives and is perhaps the most developed of all the corporate scorecard systems. During their activity-based management practice, they found that once employees were more than two levels away from the senior management, financial measures became less and less under employees' control or

Exhibit 7.2
Corporate Scorecard Perspectives with KPMs

Financial Perspective

Combined Ratio

Cash Flow

Net Fees per Employee

Return on Equity (ROE)

Economic Value Added (EVA)

Customer Perspective

Acquisition Ratio

Retention Ratio

Empathy Ratio

Responsiveness Ratio

Business Knowledge Index

Organizational Perspective

Employee Satisfaction Index Rating

Unwanted Claim/Customer Service Representative Turnover Ratio

Leadership Ratio

Operational Perspective

Use of Technology

Contested Claims

Claims Specialist Ratio

Growth and Innovation Perspective

Market Share of HMO Business

Percent of Training Goals Met

New Product Market Ratio

---

in their sight. But it was these very employees that made the products and services that enabled the company to make money. Even so, this level of performance is a lagging measure.

In the early nineties before the popularity of the Kaplan and Norton balanced scorecard, best-practices research found that there was a common set of scorecard perspectives with a common set of key performance measures. Typically, companies with corporate scorecards had four to seven perspectives, with the most common perspectives shown to the left.

Leading and Lagging Measures

A well-designed corporate scorecard has breadth, depth, and predictive power. Generally, it also has a preponderance of leading key performance measures, as opposed to trailing (historic) performance measures. Leading measures are independent variables and infrequently moderating or confounding variables. Lagging measures are usually dependent variables. Market share, a lagging measure, is a function of perceived customer value. Insurance claims processing errors, a lagging measure, is a function of the time claims representative solve problems. A recent activity-based study of nurse case managers (NCMs) in a workers compensation department revealed that the greater the detail NCMs collected about an employee's disability during the first interview, the shorter the time the employee was off the job. The reasoning is quite convincing. The more details an NCM collected about the employee, the sooner the employee had the "right" therapy and was back at work.

KPMs must maintain a consistent and corporate organizational view of performance. In physics, multilaterialism states that all functions within a system must be consistent. The same is true in a corporate scorecard. Key performance measures are often inter-related and overlapping, but they cannot be in direct opposition to one another. For example, a company cannot expect a customer service representative to

Exhibit 7.4
Corporate Scorecard Design Worksheet

Strategic Goals	Lagging Key Performance Measures	Leading Key Performance Measures	Target Measures
Financial KPMs			
• Increase the return on investment	• Combined ratio • Cash flow • Net fees per employee • Return on equity (ROE) • Economic value added (EVA)		• .176 • 356M per quarter • 18% net fee per employee • 17% • 14.3%
Customer KPMs			
• Increase customer market share	• Retention ratio • Acquisition ratio	• Customer satisfaction • Customer satisfaction	• 93% • 99%
Organizational KPMs			
• Preferred Employer • Reduce unwanted turnover	• Employee satisfaction index • Unwanted claim/CSR turnover ratio	• Management index • Management index	• >81% • <22%
Operational KPMs			
• Simplify, eliminate, automate	• Use of technology	• IT training budget	• 93% of claims handled electronically
• Reduce contested claims • Reduce operating errors	• Contested claims • Claims specialist error ratio	• Claims cycle time	• >2.6% • >2%
Growth and Innovation KPMs			
• Grow the market share • Improve employee skills	• Market share of HMO business • Percent of training goals met	• Customer value index	• >19% • >95%

solve all customer inquiries in under three minutes and simultaneously expect the same representative to solve 100% of customer concerns.

Quantitative and Qualitative Key Performance Measures

There are two basic kinds of key performance measures used in a corporate scorecard. Quantitative key performance measures are based in arithmetic and mathematics. Typically, these quantitative measures are counts, percentages, ratios, often time-bound, or have a financial nature. Qualitative key performance measures are often called soft performance measures because they are considered more subjective or perceptual in nature.[4] Employee satisfaction and customer satisfaction are the most common qualitative key performance measures.

Managers are often very resistant to including qualitative key performance measures in their balanced scorecards. Their primary fear is that employees or customers participating in surveys are often disgruntled and negative, and this will have negative effects on scorecard results. Managers' secondary fear is too much error may be associated with customer or employee satisfaction measures. But the truth is these measures are as accurate as questionnaire designers are allowed the time and money to make them. In well-designed questionnaires and decent sample sizes, customer or employee satisfaction surveys will be more accurate than most evaluations of inventory.

Managers often get themselves caught in double-speak: while they are unwilling to accept customer and employee satisfaction key performance measures in the balanced scorecard, they are almost always willing to accept similar measures or data from marketing research. From a logical and statistical point of view, managers cannot have it both ways.

Not accepting qualitative data can be detrimental to the company. In a *Fortune* 100 healthcare company, senior management decided that only "hard" output or outcome measures would be used as key performance measures in the corporate scorecard. Price premiums were used for one of the customer satisfaction key performance measures. This measure more properly belongs in either the financial or growth and innovation perspectives. The managers' refusal to use "soft" or qualitative customer key performance measures blinded them to the knowledge that customers were "leaving in droves," because claims processors lacked empathy and business knowledge and were non-responsive to complaints. In short, the corporate scorecard will not cure manager myopia. Further, the company claim representatives turnover ratio was 77% in the first year, primarily caused by incompetent first line supervisors and managers. The annual claims representative turnover cost averaged $250 million. The annual loss of customers was estimated to cost over $300 million. So much for quantitative (hard) performance measures being superior to qualitative (soft) performance measures!

There is an even more important reason to have employee and customer key performance measures in a balanced scorecard: in companies with either a customer or product strategic focus, there is a direct, mathematical relationship among employee satisfaction, customer satisfaction, and financial success. Many companies that demonstrate a gain in employee satisfaction see proportional gains in customer satisfaction and financial results.

Common Examples of Financial Key Performance Measures

- Cash flow
- Economic value added
- Return on equity
- Return on assets

While financial results remain on every company's list, there are some striking differences in what each manager thinks are the most important financial measures. In the words of Jack Welch, CEO of GE, cash flow is the pulse—the vital sign of the company. Economists support his argument that increasing cash flow is the direct result of correctly tapping the needs of the market. In the last few years, some companies have included economic value added (EVA). EVA is an index that calculates the annualized return on capital assets used by various parts of the company. The target is usually a 13.5% return on assets, roughly the cost of money and a seven% margin. Other KPMs in this list are familiar to most managers:

Common Examples of Customer Satisfaction Key Performance Measures

- Retention
- Acquisition
- Customer encounters

Customer satisfaction is the second most frequent perspective used in corporate scorecards. Like financial key performance measures, customer key performance measures evolved over the last 10 years. The acquisition and retention of customers are the most common customer key performance measures. In the not too distant past, many companies were satisfied if their employees answered their phones within three rings. While this is a very objective performance measure, it is not a customer perspective performance measure; it is an operations key performance measure. More information about customers and their needs have led to less reliance on such "objective" measures and an increased use of perceptual (leading) measures.

For example, customers' perceptions about the products and services the company provides, along with their perceptions about how they are treated, can make or break a company.

There is always a gap between a customer's expectations and his or her perception about the value of the products or services provided. Employees in contact with customers must be educated to manage that gap, and management must be held accountable for closing it. This requires the company to develop a set of performance measures that capture any contact employees have with customers. The contact can be face-to-face, by telephone, electronically by Internet, or on paper. There are five categories of customer encounter performance measures that have very effective measures of customer satisfaction:

- Keeping promises
- Ensuring that all communication is free of errors and all facilities are clean
- Increasing service providers' knowledge of products, services, and solutions to problems
- Empathizing with customers, ensuring that the company cares about them as individuals
- Responding quickly to customer problems, turning complaint-handling into a customer retention force

Common Examples of Organizational Perspective Key Performance Measures

- Leadership Quality
- Employee Satisfaction
- Use of Technology

Many companies still use the term "employee satisfaction," although the concept changed dramatically during the last 10 years. In the past, employee satisfaction focused on "hygiene factors" such as pay, insurance, physical work environment, and work rules. Hygiene factors were thought to account for a substantial portion of employee satisfaction. While hygiene factors play some role in employee satisfaction, later research reveals that employees are more motivated and committed if they have more control over work, greater contact with customers and the ability to meet their needs, and the resources that enable them to accomplish their work.[5] Since this discovery, the focus of employee satisfaction continues to change from the employee to the manager. In short, does the manager have the human resource management skills to provide her/his subordinates with the tools, resources, communication, and trust needed to accomplish the mission?

Common Examples of Operations Perspective Key Performance Measures

- Cycle time
- Process throughputs
- Transaction costs
- Process cycle times
- Customization
- Use of standardized parts
- Reduction in boundary crossings

Productivity performance measures are considerably different than those for the last 20 years. Traditionally, productivity performance measures focused on just inputs, outputs, counts (as in productivity quotas) and machine utilization. Just-in-time and new flexible factory design, coupled with activity-based costing, changed the productivity focus to total process costs (i.e., sometimes known as throughputs), process cycle time, and process set up time. In short, from large batch runs with large machines, to small, customized lot sizes for one customer, "speed" became the operative word. Productivity speed increased as the number of organizational layers decreased and the increased span of managerial control was made possible by the reduction of work.

Common Examples of Growth and Innovation Key Performance Measures

- Percent of total operating expenditures/R&D
- Percent of cross sales per customer contact
- Number of new products on market
- Training investment
- Percent market niche
- Number of new products in pipeline
- Percent of adopted employee suggestions

All companies have to be concerned about developing new products and services for the market, because they attract new customers and generate brand loyalty among long-term customers. Research clearly shows that growth and innovation are the lifelines for any market-focused company. Being able to meet customers' specialty needs is the driving force behind the product-focused strategy.

Growth and innovation have many meanings. To some companies, growth means an increase in profits, market share, and shareholder equity. To others, growth means increasing organizational and individual capability. You will need to clarify what growth means in your business and how growth supports your business strategy.

Innovation generally focuses on creating new products and services and designing new ways for work to be accomplished in a more streamlined and effective way.

Developing a Corporate Scorecard

The evolution of the corporate scorecard is an iterative process with lots of fits and starts. Don't expect the process to go smoothly; it won't. This project needs the focused attention and deliberate action of senior management. The rise and fall of their fortunes will be based on the rise and fall of the corporate scorecard results.

1. **Establish Corporate Scorecard Teams.** This is not a project you can assign to a group of eager young MBAs fresh out of their graduate program. Some consideration must be given to who is on the team; who they represent; how much support they have;

and how much they actually know about the performance measures now used by the company. In most cases, there will be an implementation team that reports to this design team.

– *The Scorecard Design Team.* Generally, senior managers have stakeholder interest in the design and use of the scorecard. This team needs the authority to determine if more than one scorecard is needed, often the case in a large diversified company.

– *The Corporate Scorecard Implementation Team.* The staff of this team supports the design team. It has representatives from Human Resources, Organizational Effectiveness, and a person with three or more semesters of statistics. The team manager needs the authority to collect any data necessary to facilitate corporate scorecard development. The statistician will prove to be invaluable in:

– Making decisions about the kinds of key performance measures used in the corporate scorecard
– Designing and implementing the computer simulations
– Establishing the validity of the scorecard

Project time varies according to the size of the organization. Our experience suggests that *Fortune* 500 companies typically require six months to a year to create KPMs and a corporate scorecard.

2. **Research.** There are many articles and books on the corporate scorecard and KPMs. Take the time to read what the articles have to say about scorecard success. This should not be a "best practices" effort. *The corporate scorecard must reflect the company's strategic focus.* The scorecard must be customized to the company. But feel free to steal any ideas that make the process easier from those that have already implemented a scorecard!

3. **Pre-meeting interviews.** Have a facilitator from outside the company conduct individual interviews with the corporate scorecard design team. The outside facilitator will bring unbiased objectivity to the interviewing process. Sixty minutes should be scheduled for each meeting, during which the meeting facilitator will use a structured interview protocol to ensure that all corporate scorecard design team managers will be asked the same questions (see pages 110–111). The protocol should:

- Cover perceived strategic focus
- Identify strategic goals
- Identify principle activity drivers
- Suggest a list of key lagging performance measures for each perspective
- Suggest a list of key leading performance measures for each perspective
- Identify perceptions of the current performance measurement systems
- Solicit feedback about the need for more than one corporate scorecard
- Solicit current perceptions about the need and use of the corporate scorecard
- Identify any resistance to the corporate scorecard

4. **Set the ground rules of developing the corporate scorecard.**

   - *Use a facilitator to run the meeting.* Egos will be involved, and emotions will run high. There needs to be a third party facilitator running the meetings. That person's objectivity and parliamentary rule will greatly speed the process.
   - *Start fresh, use a clean piece of paper.* It's best to go in without any preconceived ideas about what should or should not be in the corporate scorecard. Many managers will insist that only "hard" output or outcome measures be included in the corporate scorecard. This is very short-sighted. The most important leading key performance measures in the corporate scorecard will be employee and customer satisfaction.[6]
   - *Be realistic about needs.* Don't get hung up about the number of key performance measures in the corporate scorecard. Some companies need five, others need 25.
   - *Be realistic about data requirements.* Identify data collection needs and sources and methods of data collection.

5. **Introductory Meeting Pre-reading.** Supply each corporate scorecard design team member with the information collected during the interviews two weeks before the introductory meeting. Explain the purpose of the meeting; review the information collected thus far; and describe the outcomes of the introductory meeting.

6. **First Design Team Meeting.** This first meeting will be the most awkward and uncomfortable. The points for discussion, and for which consensus must be reached, follows:

- *Review the strategic focus.* By this time in the organizational alignment process, the senior managers should decide on the strategic focus. The discussion about strategic focus will be the most important event during any part of the development of the corporate scorecard, because it often points out some major incongruities between the various senior managers. Many managers who insist they have a customer-focused strategy are amazed to learn that quickly answering the phone is not a customer satisfaction key performance measure; it's a productivity and staffing measure.
- *Determine strategic goals.* Come to consensus about what each corporate scorecard design team member thinks are the most important or significant drivers in the company. If the company has completed an activity-based costing or management project, this should be an easy step. Use the Corporate Scorecard Design Worksheet at the end of this chapter to list the strategic goals.
- *Identify the lagging key performance measures for each perspective.* Refer to the lagging key performance measures identified in the interviews. Discuss how each supports or detracts from the strategic goals. Discuss the merits and problems with each. List the most favorable in the corporate scorecard design worksheet.
- *Identify the leading key performance measures for each perspective.* Refer to the leading key performance measures identified in the interviews. Discuss how each supports or detracts from the lagging key performance measures and/or strategic goals. Discuss the merits and problems with each. List the most favorable in the corporate scorecard design worksheet.
- *Set first year target measures.* There will be much debate about what the first year target measures should be for the corporate scorecard. The most important thing is to be willing to change them frequently if needed. List the most favorable in the corporate scorecard design worksheet.
- *Discuss data collection techniques and capability.* Determine how the corporate scorecard will be used. This is essential to the overall success of the program.

  - Will the corporate scorecard be *the* strategic performance measurement system?

      – Will it be used to make senior management compensation decisions?

      – How far down into the organization will the corporate scorecard remain unchanged?

      – When and where will changes or supplements be allowed, by whom, and when?

      – Which systems will be linked to gather performance data?

– *Discuss who will own the data.* This is a very contentious issue for every company. The answer is almost always the CFO or the COO.

7. **Consolidate Information from First Meeting.** List all the agreed upon key performance measures, issues and concerns. If possible, run computer simulations to test the validity of the corporate scorecard and financial outcomes. Report the findings to the corporate scorecard design team. Ask for feedback within two weeks.

8. **Second Design Team Meeting.** Discuss the findings in the report. If a computer simulation was developed, explain the parameters and risks of the model.[7] Run a demonstration, if asked. Ask for additional suggestions or changes. Develop a communication plan and timetable for implementation. Prepare for a middle managers meeting.

9. **Pre-reads for the Middle Managers Meeting.** Distribute findings from the second design team meeting. Discuss the findings in the report. If there were a computer model developed, explain the parameters and risks of the model. Run a demonstration, if asked. Ask for additional suggestions or changes.

10. **The Middle Manager Meeting.** During this meeting, the corporate scorecard design team will discuss:

      – How the scorecard will be used by middle management
      – The rationale for the corporate scorecard
      – The strategic goals
      – The lagging and leading key performance measures
      – The timetable for implementation
      – The depth and breadth of the roll-out
      – The expectations of middle managers
      – How the scorecard will be tied to their direct reports performance profile

11. **Linkage and Alignment.** Once the corporate scorecard has been rolled out to the middle managers, there is still more work to be done. Each middle manager must embrace the corporate scorecard and be held accountable for implementing it. Anything less will eventually undermine the meaningfulness of the scorecard. Implementation must be demanded, but how the actual results are used to make personnel decisions is a manner of corporate culture. See Chapter 10, Job and Individual Performance Measures and Management.

    Each middle manager must be able to show how any performance measures used at his/her level support one or more of the strategic goals, or lagging and leading key performance measures, used in the corporate scorecard. All other measurement systems must be eliminated from the system. This will take time. There will be disbelief that one performance measurement system is all that is needed, so shadow systems will remain or be developed. In some cases the shadow or feeder systems will be developed to support the corporate scorecard. These systems should be eliminated, and resistance to do so should be dealt with in the harshest manner. Otherwise, shadow systems will become malignant and suck valuable resources from the company.

12. **Communication.** Communicate frequently to all employees about the corporate scorecard results. Most *Fortune* 100 company managers with scorecards use them to make decisions about their company on a weekly basis. A small number of others actually run the day-to-day business operations from the scorecard results. Many *Fortune* 100 companies use their scorecard to frame all the quarterly management meetings. Others use their scorecards to communicate with all employees.

13. **Frequently Statistically Test the Scorecard.** The scorecard is worthless if it does not accurately predict, within a certain confidence level (plus or minus 2%), the financial outcomes. This is where the statisticians mentioned earlier earn their keep. Several months of data will need to be collected before any statistics can be run. But once you have 10 or more complete cycles of data (be it daily, weekly, or monthly), statistics and their significance and confidence levels can be run. Generally, the easiest statistic to run is a multiple regression equation, choosing one

Corporate Scorecard Interview Protocol

Interviewee: Interviewer:

1.	• What do you perceive as being the perceived strategy of the company?
2.	• Identify what you think are strategic goals of the company
3.	• Identify what you think are principal drivers in the company
4.	• A suggested list of lagging key performance measures for each perspective
5.	• A suggested list of leading key performance measures for each perspective

6.	• Identify perceptions of the current performance measurement systems
7.	• Solicit feedback about the need for more than one corporate scorecard
8.	• Solicit resistance to the corporate scorecard
9.	• Identify which systems should be tightly integrated with the scorecard • Integrated Financial System • Budgeting • Records • Personnel
10.	• Other suggestions or comments:

financial measure (a dependent variable) and one or more leading or lagging performance measures (the independent variables). The problem with running repetitious multiple
regression equations is that these increase the amount of aggre-
gated error. It is better to run structural equation models or
canonical correlational models for multiple dependent and independent variables.

Scorecard Caveats

Organization-wide performance measures can be tricky. There is
usually an assumption that if the underlying activities of leading key
performance measure are improved, there should be a commensurate
improvement in the lagging key performance measures (i.e., There is a
linear relationship between one and the other.) The answer is, "Well
maybe." Why? Almost all organizational key performance measures
are non-linear, curvilinear, or logistic and are part of a systems dynamic
that is multi-dimensional and highly interdependent. That means that
adding one unit of Variable A may not result in a one-unit increase in
Variable B. See Exhibit 7.5 for an illustration of the difference between
a linear relationship and a curvilinear relationship.

To Aggregate or Not to Aggregate? A primary reason that corporate
scorecards end in frustrating loggerheads is that managers insist on

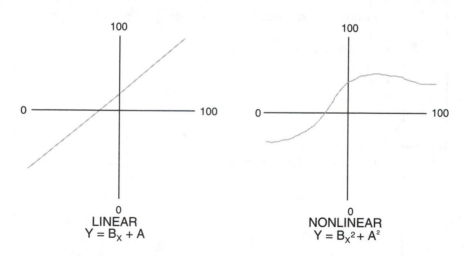

Exhibit 7.5 Linear versus Nonlinear Key Performance Measures

mathematical perfection. For example, retention of customers is critical to the insurance business, but the target measure for retention may vary widely from one line of business to the next. Aggregating customer retention ratios from all lines of business would be statistically meaningless and full of error. Some offices may need to clean their books of unprofitable policies, decreasing their retention ratio for some period of time, while other offices may actually increase their retention ratio. Exhibit 7.6 is an example of how aggregation and reporting can lead to some misunderstandings.

Exhibit 7.6
To Aggregate or Not to Aggregate?

Line of Business	Customer Retention Ratio
Line of Business A	89%
Line of Business B	61%
Line of Business C	93%
Line of Business D	92%
Aggregate	83%

In this exhibit, it appears that Line of Business B is gumming the works and having a direct impact on the customer retention ratio. But if LOB B has clean books and profitable customers, LOB B maybe the best performer of the group.

Endnotes

1. An organizational-level performance measures; key, in the sense that it is one of the most important measures within the company.

2. *The New Corporate Performance Measures.* The Conference Board, 1995.

3. Economic value added (EVA) is equivalent to a return on capital assets. It is also considered the cost of money plus any additional profit.

4. In research, qualitative information would cover any narrative, annotated, oral, visual, or conceptual data. Any scales (numerical assignations given to points on a scale) used in employee and customer satisfaction surveys are considered quantitative.

5. Gable, R., *Measuring Attitudes and Values in Corporate and School Settings.* Boston: Kluwer Academic Publishers, 1993.

The Business
Planning Process

8

Many organizations utilize specific business planning methods, such as financial gap business planning or Hoshin business planning. Typically, business plan objectives are financial or market driven. However, many companies are using the balanced scorecard along with the environmental scan, customer feedback, and organizational gap analysis to provide a broader view and deeper look at the business. The information from these sources is used to develop an activity-based business plan.

The difference between an ordinary business plan and an activity-based business plan is that many companies have only a financial business plan. Using the Typical Insurance Company, Inc. (TIC) as an example, they often look like this:

In many companies, business plans don't appear very different than the balanced sheet. This approach is carried down through the layers of the company. But there is no plan or description of what is needed to be done for the company to meet its financial objectives. Why? Many senior managers actually think that:

1. Formal descriptive business plans interfere with creativity
2. They don't want to be bothered with a detail that will have to be changed, maybe every week
3. Too many managers are tactically minded and are only concerned about this week, not next quarter

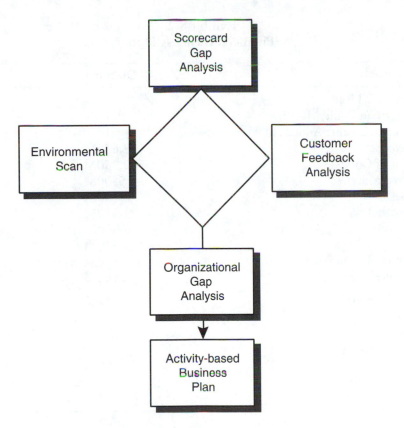

Exhibit 8.1 Business Plan Information Sources

For 10 years, TIC, Inc. had a financial objective of making double-digit returns on equity, yet it had no formalized plan to get there other than increasing market share and reducing expenses. The company never made it. Other companies adopted a Management by Objectives (MBO) approach. "Senior management will earn nine and two-tenths percent return on equity by March 31, 200X." But this did not help management meet its targets either.

The contemporary purpose of the business plan is to provide direction, accountability, and close gaps in performance. In the mid-1980s, activity-based costing (ABC) became common, and from ABC came activity-based management (ABM). The basic tenet in ABM is that companies pay for the activities performed to build the products and services sold; resources are allocated to these activities; and, therefore, these activ-

Exhibit 8.2
Financial Business Plan

Financials	Objectives
Combined Ratio	91%
Return on Equity (ROE)	17%
Economic Value Added (EVA)	14.3%
Revenue	$2,650M
Cost of Goods	$2,250M
Gross Margin	$400M
Sales	$100M
Distribution	$70M
Finance	$70M
IT	$60M
Human Resources	$20M
Income	**$80M**
Market Share	27%
ROI	4.4%
Price/Book	1.05
Price/Earning	13.15%
Price/Sales	67%
Return on Assets	9.2%
Return on Equity	8.13%

ities will be managed better. An activity-based business plan has five major components: the activity performed, the outcome of that activity, the target measures used to assess the effort or the outcome, the data sources used to make that assessment, and the owner. See Exhibit 8.3.

The power of activity-based management soon was married with Hoshin business planning cycle (plan, do, assess, revise), and a very powerful business planning tool was born. The remainder of this chapter will describe how to build an activity-based business plan using the various sources of business information.

Corporate Scorecard Gap Analysis. The most recent addition to developing a business plan is the corporate scorecard. The *difference* between the balanced scorecard results and the established target measures is subtle but can be a major source of business information. There are some questions of *why* a difference is necessary.

Exhibit 8.3
The Component of an Activity-Based Business Plan

Activities
- What is to be done

Outcomes
- The result of that effort

Target Measures
- Performance measures

Data Source
- What information will be used to assess the effort and outcome

Owner
- Who will be responsible for completing the activity and the quality of the outcome

1. How does present performance contrast with balanced scorecard targets?
2. In activity terms, why are there reasons for not achieving balanced scorecard targets?
3. Which activities need reinforcing to close gaps between balanced scorecard results and targets?
4. What is a root cause analysis for the differences?

The first question is, "How did TIC do compared to their balanced scorecard?" For that, we need to refine the balanced scorecard table in Exhibit 8.4.

From comparing the balanced scorecard target measures to actual performance, we see that seven areas need management's attention. These seven areas will be the gaps that must be closed.

1. The combined ratio actual was 95.5%, compared to the target of 91%
2. The EVA actual was 12.1%, compared to the target of 14.3%
3. The retention ratio actual was 91.7%, compared to the target of 14.3%
4. Unwanted turnover was 25%, compared to the target of 22%
5. The leadership ratio was 81%, compared to the target of 86%

Exhibit 8.4
The Typical Insurance Company's Balanced Scorecard

Perspective/ Key Performance Measures	Lagging KPMs	Leading KPMs	Actuals	Rating
Financial Perspective				
Combined Ratio	91%		95.5%	Th
Cash Flow	365 per quarter		365 3rd quarter	T
Net Fees per Employee	$6,435		$6,565	T1
Return on Equity (ROE)	17%		17.1%	T
Economic Value Added (EVA)	14.3%		12.1	Th
Customer Perspective				
Retention Ratio	93.5%		91.7	Th
Customer Satisfaction Index Rating		99%	99.2	T
Organizational Perspective				
Employee Satisfaction Rating		>81%	88%	T1
Unwanted CSR Turnover Ratio		<22%	25%	Th
Leadership Ratio		>86%	81%	Th
Operational Perspective			−93%	
Percent electronic claims		>2.6%	293.1%	T
Contested Claims		>2%	2.6%	T
Specialist Claim Ratio			2.6%	Th
Growth and Innovation				
Market Share of HMO Business	>19%		19.1	T
Percent of Training Goals Met		>95%	93%	Th

Th = Threshold   = 80–90% of Target
T2 = Target minus   = 91–95% of Target
T = Target   = 96–104% of Target
T1 = Target plus   = 105–114% of Target
S2 = Superior minus = 115–124% of Target
S = Superior   = 125–135% of Target
S1 = Superior plus   = > 135% of Target

6. The specialty claim ratio was 2.6%, compared to the target of 2%
7. Only 93% of the training goals were met, compared to the target of 95%

A root cause analysis of each of these gaps would be performed where possible. Trying to conduct a root cause analysis on the combined ratio would be silly because all of the other balanced scorecard key performance measures lead to this one measure. The root causes would be expressed in the actions needed to close the gaps and entered into the business plan. This process would be continued for the organizational gap analysis, the environmental scan, and the customer feedback analysis.

Environmental Scan

The purpose of the environmental scan is to:

- Assess environment for existing products/services
- Identify current and potential customers
- Identify new products/services from other industries
- Look at what's happening internationally
- Identify non-customers
- Look far into future (e.g., growing wood in shape of furniture)

The environmental scan is conducted using market research, industry journals, futurist news letters, trade shows, newspapers, suppliers, supplier's suppliers, customers, and hired competitive intelligence. Let's assume that a thorough environmental scan has been done, and the result is the following list of gaps:

1. The property and casualty products were more difficult to buy than from competitors.
2. The property and casualty products, on the average, cost 6.7% more than the market average.
3. Property and casualty complaint handling was completed by competitors in less time. Most competitors had fewer screens, with more information on them, than our system.
4. Property and casualty sales costs were 4.7% higher than the mean.
5. TIC has no presence in the growing personal watercraft property and casualty market.

Customer Feedback

The dual purpose of the customer feedback analysis is to assess satisfaction with existing products/services and to estimate the probability of the same customer purchasing the same product or a similar product the company offers. Customer feedback on the following is critical:

- Identifying customer and product/service attributes
- Identifying new products/services requested
- Identifying and prioritizing problems/issues that arise
- Ensuring issues are logged into the system
- Ensuring that trends are identified, reported, and solved
- Pinpointing customer encounters
- Identifying where encounters occur
- Determining what interactions are most important
- Assessing employee business knowledge at the point of the encounter
- Assessing employee's urgency to solve customer complaints
- Assessing the degree to which the employee entered accurate information into the system
- Identifying performance that should be rewarded

Tools used to collect customer feedback include:

- Customer logs
- Surveys
- Interviews
- Focus groups
- Professional association feedback
- Mystery shoppers

Assume the following gaps were developed from the customer feedback analysis:

1. Customer wants one point of contact for complaints.
   a) One 800 number
   b) One touch number for property and casualty, one touch for mutual funds

2. Customer wants one person to handle his complaints
   a) One customer service representative to handle the case
   b) One supervisor to handle the case

	C	A
High Priority	One point of contact for complaints	One CSR
Low Priority	D One touch number	B One supervisor
	Short term	Long term

Exhibit 8.5 *Customer Feedback Analysis*

Organizational Gap Analysis

The purpose of the organizational gap analysis is to examine the company's internal capability of meeting the demands of strategy implementation. Some possible examples of opportunities can be found by:

- Identifying architectural misalignments
- Judging cross-functional cooperation
- Judging vertical efficiency
- Judging horizontal efficiency
- Looking far into future for possible R&D projects

Components of an Activity-Based Business Plan

A business plan is just another kind of performance measurement tool; this one is used for assessing the gaps during the performance

Gap Size/ Priority	High	Medium	Low
Large	Too many layers of management	Sr. management does not model new roles	Administration policies don't allow employees flexibility
Medium	Quality not integrated into planning process	Employees lack customer service skills	
Small	Employees not rewarded for teamwork		Current information system batch driven

Exhibit 8.6 Organizational Gap Analysis

year. But there are some fundamental differences between a typical business plan and an activity-based business plan. First and foremost, the activity-based business plan covers all the activities identified in the gap and root cause analyses. Second, it covers the outcomes of each activity. Third, it has target performance measures for the activity, the outcome, or both. Fourth, it lists the data sources used to judge an employee's performance. Fifth, it identifies who is responsible for each activity.

Perspectives

Each activity-based business plan should contain the same perspective as those listed in the corporate scorecard (e.g., financial, customer, organizational, operational, growth and innovation perspectives, and business objective sections). These perspectives often contain a set of measures from the corporate scorecard to be shared by all employees. This effort links the business plan to the business strategy. The following are the minimum requirements for a successful activity-based business plan:

- *Financial Perspective.* In this section the manager and his or her immediate supervisor negotiates the financial outcome of the manager's unit.

Exhibit 8.7
Components of an Activity-Based Business Plan

Perspectives/Activities	Outcomes	Target Measures	Data Source	Owner
Financial Perspective				
Decrease combined ratio		88.5%	Financial reports	Senior management
Increase EVA		14.5%	Financial reports	Senior management
Customer Perspective				
Increase customer retention ratio	Stable customer base	94%	CSI report	Senior management
Increase customer satisfaction ratio	Loyal customer base	99%	CSI report	All employees
Organizational Perspective				
Increase Employee Satisfaction Index	Committed employees	>81%	ESI report	Senior and middle managers
Reduce unwanted claim employee turnover	Reduced turnover costs	<22%	ESI report	Senior and middle managers
Increase Leadership Index		>86%	ESI report	
Operational Perspective				
Growth & Innovation Perspective				

Financial target measures may include combined ratios, expenses, economic value added, return on assets, return on benefits, etc.

- *Customer Perspective.* This section focuses on increasing customer satisfaction with the overall goal of retaining current customers. Some possible activities to be addressed are increasing the measurement of customer encounters; developing a customer satisfaction index; and tracking product features that customers find valuable.

- *Organizational Perspective.* The organizational perspective identifies leadership, management, employee, technological architecture, and organizational structure activities that are critical to the success of the organization. Such activities include increasing teamwork and cooperation, developing the overall quality of leadership skills, increasing the degree and quality of communications, developing people, and improving performance management. The organizational perspective could also have activities addressing the technological architecture.

- *Operational Perspective.* Operational excellence is primarily concerned with improvements in cost, cycle time, conformance to standards, quantity, and quality. Overlaps often occur between operational excellence and other sections, such as customer satisfaction, where solving a customer problem efficiently increases productivity.

- *Growth and Innovation Perspective.* Each employee is accountable for continuous improvement of the business and himself, as well as the adoption and diffusion of innovations and improvements. This ensures that each employee understands and is rewarded for continuous improvement and innovation.

Content of Each Column in the Performance Profile

- *Activities.* Activities are the behaviors that a company pays an employee to exhibit. These are objectives, tasks, action steps, or other behaviors such as competencies. The list of activities is long and varied. But all activities in a business plan should be under the direct control of the employee. Each activity culminates in an output, or what we call a "deliverable."

- *Outcomes.* Each activity has an end outcome, product, or service. The activity "empathizing with the customer" has as its output a satisfied customer. While this seems self-evident, most managers are surprised when going through this exercise that many employees do not understand or identify with the outcome.

- *Target Measures.* Target measures are the performance standards used for an activity, a deliverable, or both. The activity "empathizing with the customer" can be measured by the use of effective customer service language or the satisfaction of the customer. Typically, target measures are expressed in ratios, such as "reduced waste 23% in three months," and "increased customer satisfaction in six weeks."

- *Data Sources.* The data source column identifies where performance data information will be gathered from and/or by whom it will be gathered. The data source for *teamwork and cooperation* could be observation by team members or citations from team members, and feedback from managers. Logs, audits, reports, surveys, and counts are also data sources.

- *Rating.* The results column indicates the degree to which an individual achieved an objective, performed the job's fundamental components, or met human resource and financial performance measures by the use of a scale. The scales should be appropriate to the performance measure, much like the scale used below.

Th = Threshold   = 80–90% of Target
T2 = Target minus   = 91–95% of Target
T = Target   = 96–104% of Target
T1 = Target plus   = 105–114% of Target
S2 = Superior minus = 115–124% of Target
S = Superior   = 125–135% of Target
S1 = Superior plus   = >135% of Target

Summary

The contemporary purpose of the activity-based business plan is to provide direction and accountability, and to close gaps in performance. In the mid-1980s activity-based costing (ABC) became common, and from ABC came activity-based management (ABM). The basic tenet in ABM is that companies pay for the activities performed to build the products and services sold; resources are allocated to these activities; because of this, these activities will be managed better.

- Many managers are using the balanced scorecard along with the environmental scan, customer feedback, and organizational gap analysis to provide a broader view and deeper look at the business.

- Managers that have developed scorecards, or used activity-based costing, have discovered that they must manage the activities of their companies before they will get the desired results.

- These same managers use the same perspective in their business plan as used in their scorecards. This eliminates confusion from among the different documents.

Exhibit 8.8

The Components of an Activity-Based Business Plan

Perspectives/Activities	Outcomes	Target Measures	Data Source	Rating
Financial Perspective				T
Decrease combined ratio		88.5%	Financial reports	T
Increase EVA		14.5%	Financial reports	T
Customer Perspective				T–
Increase customer retention ratio	Stable customer base	94%	CSI report	T–
Increase customer satisfaction ratio	Loyal customer base	99%	CSI report	T–
Organizational Perspective				T+
Increase Employee Satisfaction Index	Committed employees	>81%	ESI report	T+
Reduce unwanted claim employee turnover	Reduced turnover costs	<22%	ESI report	T+
Increase Leadership Index		>86%	ESI report	T+
Operational Perspective				
Growth & Innovation Perspective				

Process Performance Measures

9

There are several different definitions of processes and process decomposition hierarchies employed in the business world. Exhibit 9.1 illustrates the process decomposition hierarchies commonly used by individuals who adhere to a reengineering, activity-based management and industrial/organizational view of business.

Definition of a Process

A process is a series of activities that transform an input into an output—a product or service. Examples of a process include the completion of a sales order, the development of a sales report, or the fabrication of a radio. This definition implies that all processes are discrete. In manufacturing this may be true, but determining the boundaries of a process can turn into a territorial dispute between corporate staff processes. No matter how one defines a process, a process should be judged by what it contributes to achieving the business strategy. It is no longer acceptable to ask how a process contributes value to just the customer, which is a major theme in Total Quality Management (TQM), because the customer may not be the primary factor in the business strategy.

Some significant advances have been made since the beginning of TQM. Activity-based costing and activity-based management (ABM) has made it possible to allocate costs and value to specific functions or processes, greatly increasing the reliability and validity of financial information at their origin. Just as importantly, ABM made it possible to more easily identify and implement process performance measures.

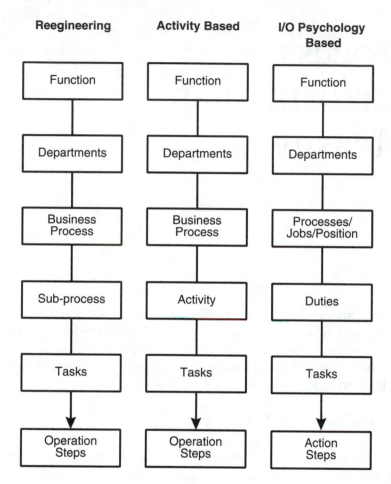

Reengineering	Activity Based	I/O Psychology Based
Function	Function	Function
Departments	Departments	Departments
Business Process	Business Process	Processes/ Jobs/Position
Sub-process	Activity	Duties
Tasks	Tasks	Tasks
Operation Steps	Operation Steps	Action Steps

Exhibit 9.1 Defining Processes

Most organizations have "functional-level" business units such as sales and marketing, operations, or human resources. In sales and marketing there are several processes such as market research, 1-800 sales, and direct sales. Each of these processes contains specific jobs, and each job is composed of one or more duties, such as customer order completion in a 1-800 sales job and shipping.

Each duty is composed of tasks. For the 1-800 sales duty of customer order completion, the tasks are to greet the customer; elicit each item to be purchased; verify the item's in-stock-status; complete and verify payment information; complete and verify shipping information, repeating all pertinent information; and estimating date of shipping and date of arrival.

Types of Process Performance Measures

Process performance measures form a bridge that links functional measures and individual and job outcome measures. There are four types of process performance measures:

1. *End of process*. These measures focus on the final product/ service that is being delivered. They typically originate directly from your customer's requirements.
2. *Functional boundaries*. Most processes touch several different functions. Think of a process as a line of people who are passing a baton to each other. Every time the baton is passed, there is a potential for it to be dropped. Research indicates that problems frequently occur at the point of interface, and metrics should be put in place to identify and address these problems.
3. *Major sub-products*. All processes deliver a final product or service. Most of these are comprised of one or more sub-products/ services. It is extremely useful to identify problems as soon as possible in order to take corrective actions.
4. *Variances*. A variance is any unplanned event. It is the delta between what you wanted and what you actually delivered. Most processes have natural "break points." By using metrics at these break points, problems can be more easily identified and corrected.

When developing measures, we recommend starting from the end of the process and developing specific metrics that evaluate how well you are delivering the processes, final products, or services. Additional metrics should be developed at key points where the process crosses functional boundaries, where major sub-products are produced, and where quality problems frequently occur in the process.

What Do You Measure?

Once an organization has defined the process boundaries, measuring the process and its outcomes is usually much easier. Almost every process can be measured using one to five categories of performance measures:

1. Cycle time
2. Costs
3. Quantity

4. Quality
5. Customer user standards

Some would argue that customer service/satisfaction is a subset of quality. That may be true, but customer service/satisfaction is always one of the categories in a balanced scorecard. To imply it has lesser status at the process level seems to defeat the purpose of the balanced scorecard. There are more detailed examples of each of the five categories of process-level performance measures:

1. **Cycle Time.** Cycle time process performance metrics measure the total elapsed time to complete a specific process. If a process starts at 8:01 and ends at 9:23 the cycle time is 82 minutes. Exhibit 9.2 represents a 1-800 customer ordering process. Cycle time begins when the 1-800 customer service representative answers the phone and ends when the goods are loaded on the delivery truck.

   The cycle time for the 1-800 Customer Service Process is calculated by adding the time it takes to complete all the discrete activities, or *the process,* as denoted by the task boxes. The information

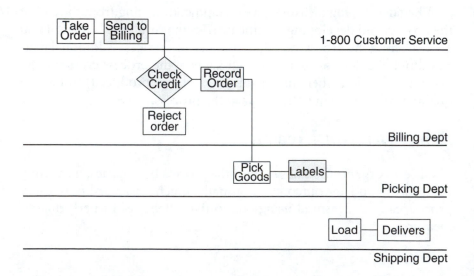

Exhibit 9.2 1-800 Customer Service Map

from the map is transferred to a spreadsheet for time and costs to be calculated. See Exhibit 9.3.

Most companies employ simple methods of calculating cycle time. The most frequently used method is called "work sampling." In this approach, employees are asked to keep accurate records of the time it takes them to complete a discrete activity such as taking an order. As Exhibit 9.4 indicates, the data is collected and entered into a spreadsheet to calculate average times and standard deviations.

Work sampling has some downsides. Workers are often less than enthusiastic to take on additional tasks. Further, work sampling is often seen as an attempt to increase "line speed," (i.e., increasing the speed in which workers have to complete a given process) and this sometimes produces inaccurate data. The solution is to continue sampling work until there is adequate confidence in the data. Be sure to point out to employees that inaccurate or unreliable information will only result in another round of data gathering. Finally, work sampling can be costly.

To address these problems with work sampling, many companies are videotaping employees performing their jobs. Full notification is given to employees before the project starts. Videotaping seems less intrusive to employees than work sampling. They soon forget about the presence of cameras, increasing the reliability of the data collected. The videotape is then viewed and average times are calculated. Many companies find that hiring undergraduate engineering students is an inexpensive means to watch the videotapes and record the data.

2. **Cost.** Process costs are calculated by aggregating all costs within a process. This includes labor and benefits, depreciation of machinery, cost of materials, allocation of any information technology costs, rent, utilities, and the cost of money for the capital allocation. This is often referred to as "fully-loaded-labor-costs" (FLLC). In Exhibit 9.3, the FLLC of each task is calculated. The average cost for this process is $11.92.

3. **Quantity.** Quantity process performance measures usually count the number of widgets, the number of gadgets, and the number of claims processed within a certain amount of time. Quantity is an important measure, but it has to be tempered with the quality of the item being produced. We have all learned since the 1970s that customers demand quality goods and service; producing inferior quality widgets for which there is no market makes no business sense.

Exhibit 9.3
Activity-Based Costing: The 1-800 Customer Service Process

Stake Holders	A1	A2	A3	A4	A5	A6	A7	A8	
Customer 1-800-777-7777									
CSR	Take order	Send to billing							
Billing			Check credit	Record order					
Picking					Pick order	Label			
Transportation							Load	Ship	
Time and dollar standards									
Mean time per order in seconds	540	4	240	60	300	120	480		Process Cycle Time 1744
Mean fully-loaded labor cost per activity	$3.69	$0.03	$1.64	$0.41	$2.05	$0.82	$3.28		Process Costs $11.92

Exhibit 9.4
Work Sampling Table

Customer encounter events (CEE)	A1	A2	A3	A4	A5	A6	A7	A8
1	0.12	0.01	0.07	0.12	0.18	0.20		20.00
2	0.12	0.02	0.08	0.12	0.18	0.02		24.00
3	0.13	0.02	0.09	0.12	0.16	0.02		25.00
4	0.13	0.02	0.09	0.13	0.16	0.02		26.00
5	0.13	0.02	0.10	0.13	0.15	0.02		35.00
6	0.14	0.03	0.10	0.14	0.15	0.03		36.00
7	0.14	0.03	0.10	0.14	0.14	0.03		36.00
8	0.14	0.03	0.10	0.14	0.14	0.03		37.00
9	0.14	0.04	0.10	0.14	0.14	0.04		38.00
10	0.15	0.04	0.11	0.15	0.14	0.04		39.00
11	0.15	0.04	0.11	0.15	0.13	0.04		41.00
12	0.16	0.04	0.11	0.16	0.13	0.04		43.00
13	0.16	0.05	0.12	0.16	0.13	0.05		44.00
14	0.18	0.05	0.12	0.18	0.12	0.05		45.00
15	0.19	0.06	0.13	0.19	0.12	0.06		48.00
Mean TTCO	0.15	0.03	0.10	0.14	0.14	0.05		35.80
SD TTCO	0.02	0.01	0.02	0.02	0.02	0.04		8.44
Performance standard (1/21.5 SDs) in hours	0.12–0.18	0.15–0.45	0.07–0.12	0.13–0.17	0.12–0.175	0.035–0.065		23.5–33.5

4. **Quality.** Quality is usually measured by the degree to which you meet the customer's desired product/service attributes. Attributes vary according to the product/service being delivered. Examples of commonly measured attributes include functionality, error rate, and performance to schedule. Standards are usually for the degree of quality expected. Manufacturers commonly use what is called the Six Sigma Standard, or less than one bad part in a million. No strenuous quality standards are adopted in the service industry but the cry for "zero defects" is heard in the hallways. See Chapter 10, Job and Individual Performance Measures and Management, about combining quantity and quality measures into a quality performance index.

5. **Conformance to User Standards: Service Level Agreements and Standard Operating Procedures.** Every process has handoffs (inputs and outputs). The users of the products are affected by the quality of those products and services. Employees expect their checks to be accurate, information technology teams expect to get accurate specifications from management about the programs they want developed, and clients expect their records to be current. Furthermore, companies rely more than ever on cross-functional cooperation to make the businesses productive. One of the ways to insure that these functions run as smoothly as possible is to develop service level agreements and standard operating procedures.

A service level agreement explicitly states in writing the objectives, roles, responsibilities, timing, and quality of handoffs within or between organizations. The rationale for developing service level agreements is listed in Exhibit 9.5. Service level agreements have specific components that make them useful tools for managing processes. Exhibit 9.6 presents some common components of a service level agreement.

Exhibit 9.5
Customer Service Level Agreement Between Process Objectives

- The implementation of accountability
- Who is required to do what, by when, and to what degree
- The number of changes made to documents
- On-time schedules and schedule adherence by work
- Customer service level, past due orders, and lost sales reports
- Work order completion report

Exhibit 9.6
Service Level Agreement Form

Service Objectives	To establish, decrease the amount of time spent correcting benefits and payroll deduction errors, and to reduce the number of boundary crossings between payroll and HR customer service representatives.
Parties	Those involved in this service agreement
Points of Contact	Location of the handoffs and the people, systems, or organizations involved
Activities	Activities being performed
Deliverables	The products, goods, or services provided
Performance Measures	Performance measures used to evaluate the activities or deliverables
Data Sources	Information sources used to make the evaluation
Work Flow	The work flow between different parties
Service Levels	The performance guarantees made by each party
Renegotiating Terms	Rules for when and how this agreement can be amended
Enforcement	The person responsible for enforcing the SLA

Standard Operating Procedures

Standard operating procedures (SOPs) were quite prevalent until the mid 1970s, when it was thought that SOPs stifled employee creativity. But with the increased focus on customers in the late 1980s, fully scripted standards for customer service representative interactions with customers became ubiquitous. Standard operating procedures are simply a description of the way a process will be performed by every employee. We are listing here standard formats for developing SOPs for the Service Center. Please note that there are two formats.

Conventional Standard Operating Procedures

All conventional SOPs should contain all of the following:

Description	The description section names the procedure, identifies what initiates the procedure,

	and provides a general description of the roles and responsibilities of each individual involved in the procedure.
Procedure Detail	This section provides a detailed narrative and/or graphic description of the procedure. The detail must be sufficient for most individuals to know how to accomplish the procedure with minimal help.
Security Issues	This section describes any security issues that are manifested in the procedures, such as password, access privileges, access timing.
Audit Requirements	In some procedures, it is necessary to *separate duties* within the procedure. For example, when a non-active employee remits a check to HRS Finance for benefits payment, the check is posted by one individual and confirmed by another.
Compliance Issues	In some procedures it is necessary to meet legally mandated, recommended, or suggested requirements within the procedure. For instance, only some individuals may have access to medical information, depending on compliance requirements of the procedures.
Additional Information	This section provides any additional information a Service Center Associate may want or need to complete the procedure. This should include specialists, telephone numbers, and Intranet or Internet sites.

Benefits Retroactive Processing Example

Description

As a result of Valid Family Status Changes, a report is generated to capture deductions for benefits that were updated to the Human Resources system. The associate must validate that the retroactive amounts are correct and determine if corrective action is necessary.

Procedure Detail

1. Generate a retroactive benefits report on a daily basis.
2. Validate the retroactive amount by matching coverage with YTD deduction balance panel and/or employee balance review (from administer billing panel). The job data one panel must be utilized to view prior/current status to determine what YTD panels will verify the deduction. If the deduction balance in both panels corresponds to the benefit effective date, go to Manage Retroactive Processing, select Retro-Benefits-Review and Update panel, "calculate" (hit enter to bring record up). Click off "OK to Process" for each benefit by pay period so that the amount will not be taken again from the employee's next pay check.
3. If deduction balance does not match coverage and the retroactive amount is credit or a debit, you must research to determine if the credit/debit is valid. (Check Job Data to determine what might have caused this retro-benefits process.)
4. If the credit or debit is valid, let the Retro-Benefits process run so the employee will receive a refund or additional charge on the paycheck. If the credit or debit is not valid, go to Manage Retroactive Processing and select Retro-Benefits Review and Update panel (enter employee ID, select "calculate," and click off "OK to Process" button). This will stop the Retro-Benefits process. If the Retro-Benefits amount should be different from the amount the system calculated, override the amount, enter the correct deduction on the "Override Deduction Amount" box, and save. The override will take precedent over the Retro-Benefits deduction amount calculated by the system.

Suggestions

New Query
- Develop a query to eliminate unnecessary data from the report (current report extremely lengthy 400 to 500 pages). The query would include only debits/credits in employee ID order. A query that runs against cash billing identifies all employees that were out on a leave who have made payments. Human Resources will eliminate unnecessary data on the report.

Parking Lot Issues
- Can the right queries be written that will enhance the process?
- Experts on Retro-Benefits Process are part of Financial, not the HR Service Center.

Three Ways to Develop Process Performance Measures

Process performance measures should not stand alone nor is there a need to use techniques separate from those used for continuous process improvement or reengineering. The three basic approaches to developing process performance measures are:

- Process maps
- Activity charts
- Task analyses

Process maps

Process maps are an excellent source of performance measures. Managers are advised to take the next steps and use process maps to help them develop performance measures. Unfortunately, many of the process maps do not provide the necessary depth and breadth of information that managers need to make good business decisions. Most are drawn on one page for convenience, but suffer from too much detail. Thus the name "spaghetti charts" is often applied to this mishmash of inter-tangled information. Process maps are made more intelligible and more useful, for both productivity improvement and performance measures, by following some simple mapping rules.

Basic discipline is needed to develop process maps. Exhibit 9.7 presents a summary table of the steps to process mapping and information sources.

- Map from customer to the job that is most critical to the customer, to other supporting jobs, indicating boundary crossings (jobs, departments, organizations, as shown in Exhibit 9.8).
- Map the tasks in processes from left to right, following the continuum of time. Any tasks that appear under each other indicate that they can be undertaken in the same time frame or simultaneously.

Short-Term Disability Paper Work Process (With Screen Display)

Description

Employee verifying whether a check is issued after return from short-term disability

Procedure Detail

1. Open People Soft Work Force Job Data 1
2. Verify status on file: active, inactive
3. Verify effective date
4. Verify keyed date
5. Is current status showing employee active?
   - If no, then advise employee return to work information not yet keyed or in system
     - If not in system, refer to WCDS
     - Log into Expert Advisor
     - Terminate call
   - If yes, advise employee information is in the system, supply effective date and date keyed
6. Was information keyed in time to be reflected in current check?
   - If no, advise employee any adjustments owed will be in next check
     - Log into Expert Advisor
     - Terminate call
   - If yes, advise employee any adjustment owed will be in this check
     - Log into Expert Advisor
     - Terminate call

Security Issues Need to verify ID, social security number, and cost center before providing information

Audit Requirements None

Compliance Issues See security issues, abide by the rules of confidentiality

Additional Information May confirm adjustments are included in current check by accessing paycheck data in People Soft Compensate

Exhibit 9.7
Steps and Information Sources Used in Process Mapping

Steps	Information Sources
Map from the customer down	Customer, stake holders
Identify process starts and stops	Process owners
Identify activities (tasks) and boundary crossings	Stake holders
Identify hand-offs and bottlenecks	Stake holders
Estimate the cost of each activity (task)	Finance, stake holder
Standardize performance measures	Management, process owners

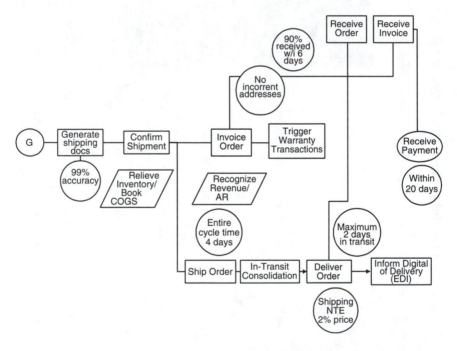

Exhibit 9.8 Example of a Process Map with End of Process, Variance, and Functional Measures

Once you have mapped a process, you have identified the process's essential activities. Exhibit 9.9 is an activity and performance table that examines the 1-800 sales process mapped above by cycle time, cost to the company to perform the activity, conformance to customer standards,

Exhibit 9.9
1-800 Sales Activity and Performance Table

Task/Activity	Deliverable	Customer Measures	Quality	Quantity	Mean Cycle Time	Cost/$*
Take order	Completed order	Customer empathy Product knowledge	100% accuracy	>60 tpd/CSR*	7.5 minutes	1.25
Credit check	Approved credit		100% correct approval	60 tpd/CSR	0.03 minutes	0.49
Billing	Automated transfer		100% accuracy	60 tpd/CSR	0.03 minutes	0.49
Pick goods	Packaged order		100% accuracy	>90	4.5 minutes	0.75
Label package	Ready to ship package		100% accuracy	>280	1.5 minutes	0.25
Delivery	Satisfied customer	Empathy		>60 tpd	<48 hours	3.15
					13.56	6.38

*Assume $10.00 simple labor; allocations, depreciation, and contracted delivery costs
** tpd = transactions per day

quality, and quantity. This is often referred to as the activity and performance table. It is important to note that not all cells in the activity and performance table need to be completed. In fact, some redundancy often exists between two or more categories.

Labor costs can be examined from a simple cost per labor hour, the wage paid to an employee to perform a task in a process, or the more accurate fully-loaded activity cost (FLAC).[1] There is a significant difference between the two cost calculations. See Exhibit 9.10. In the simple method only the actual hourly wage is calculated, although at some companies there is the added cost of benefits. Companies involved in activity-based management calculate all it takes to support an employee to perform a specific activity (read: process). This detailed picture of costing every element in a process provides a more accurate calculation of actual process costs as compared to the more traditional allocation accounting structure.[2]

Most world-class manufacturing companies have discovered that the tracking of labor costs does not meet their information needs because it does not provide a comprehensive picture of what actual costs are on the factory floor. Activity-based management advocates would rather calculate the total cost of performing a specific activity. This calculation could include not only wage and benefit costs but also personal computer depreciation, IT allocation, equipment and furniture depreciation, the cost of space (rent), and transportation costs.

Therefore, the cost column in Exhibit 9.10 varies greatly depending on whether simple labor costs or fully loaded activity cost methods are used. If you are interested in FLAC, it helps to bring in someone from

Exhibit 9.10
Simple vs. Fully Loaded Activity Costs

	Simple Labor Calculation	Fully Loaded Calculation
Hourly wage	10.00	10.00
Benefits	2.50	2.50
PC depreciation		0.35
IT allocation		0.10
Furniture		0.25
Rent		6.00
Transportation		0.45
Costs	12.50	19.65

the finance department to help get you started. In short, developing simple process maps can help identify the important activities within a process. Once the map is developed, the identified activities are used to develop an activity and performance table.

Activity charts

Activity charts (also called function charts, entity charts, or relationship charts) show the relationship between each activity performed in a process and its relationship between the people, systems, or organizations within the company. The chart is a simple table format but can often be pages long. Exhibit 9.11 uses the 1-800-Sales organization example.

Activity charts provide more explicit information about a process and, consequently a more encompassing set of performance measures are developed. But the amount of information is sometimes overwhelming if you use these charts to create performance measures for individuals. For help in overcoming this task, see Chapter 10, "Job and Individual Performance Measures and Management."

In most companies the primary consideration is delivering the service/product on time, without complications to the customer. Most processes have some redundancy between customer service (or end user) measures and quality measures. That is to be expected, but detailing them is critical to ensure the employee understands the importance of these measures. In the earlier example it's important to note that the employee has limited or no control over system interfaces. That is, the employee cannot make the order input system go faster. However, good employees can often find ways to increase their speed by learning ways of reducing the number of "screens" accessed to input customer information, reducing the amount of time it takes to complete an order. The added detail that activity charts supply can often help a company pinpoint a more comprehensive set of customer service performance measures, as seen in Exhibit 9.9.

Most importantly, activity charts accurately detail the myriad system organizations, vendors, and people that a single process touches. Further, activity charts are used to identify and later reduce the number of boundary crossings within an organization. When combined with process maps, they become invaluable management tools. For example, a finance department had many contacts with health and wealth benefits, often shuffling paper among the three departments and some vendors. The activity charts helped the company staff to design a benefits

Exhibit 9.11
1-800-Sales Activity Chart

Activity/Relationship	Customer	Order Entry System	Credit System	Billing System	Picking	Shipping
Take customer order	• Greet customer • Ask for first and last name • Ask for order • Ask for item characteristics • Ask for credit/ATM card # • Verify card # • State order number • Inquire about additional items • Offer sales items • Indicate delivery dates • Thank customer for order	• Log in names • Check availability • Log-in order • Verify order # of screen accessed	• Input card number • Verify card number • Verify credit availability			
Billing System				• Receive order billing • Order sent to Picking		
Pick goods					• Pick and pack order • Check order for completeness	
Label package					• Compare packing slip to order • Verify order number and packing slip • Pack order • Pack order • Move to shipping	
Deliver Order						• Load within 24 hours • Ship within 36

1-800-Sales	Task Symbols*
Greet customer	● ▷ ☐ △ ▽
Ask for first and last name	● ▷ ☐ △ ▽
Ask for order	● ▷ ☐ △ ▽
Ask for item characteristics	● ▷ ☐ △ ▽
Ask for credit/ATM card #	○ ▷ ☐ △ ▼
Verify card #	○ ▷ ☐ ▲ ▽
State order number	● ▷ ☐ △ ▽
Inquire about additional items	● ▷ ☐ △ ▽
Offer sales items	● ▷ ☐ △ ▽
Indicate delivery dates	● ▷ ☐ △ ▽
Thank customer for order	● ▷ ☐ △ ▽
Pick and pack order	○ ▷ ■ △ ▽
Check order for completeness	○ ▷ ☐ ▲ ▽
Compare packing slip to order	○ ▷ ☐ ▲ ▽
Verify order number and packing slip	○ ▷ ☐ ▲ ▽
Pack order	○ ▷ ■ △ ▽
Meet packing standards	○ ▷ ☐ ▲ ▽
Move to shipping	○ ▶ ☐ △ ▽
Ship	○ ▶ ☐ △ ▽
Inquire/State =	○
Transport =	▷
Perform =	☐
Inspect =	△
Input =	▽

Exhibit 9.12 1-800-Sales Task Analysis

service center by organizing all benefits processing within one unit. The reorganization also made a substantial contribution to the company through the redeployment of several middle managers and processing employees while increasing customer satisfaction. The activity charts also identified tasks that could be eliminated or changed to be less onerous to management and employees. The net savings of the reorganization were over $2 million with the added bonus of increased customer satisfaction.

Task analyses

Task analysis provides a comprehensive list of task-level detail and presents a graphic illustration of how work flows across a process. But task analysis doesn't add any additional information about the process itself. There are standard task symbols promoted by many associations and consulting firms. Feel free to use them. Many companies end up developing their own set of symbols. Many presentation and flow-charting software packages have a set of symbols that can be easily adapted. The important thing is to *standardize these symbols across the company.*

Which Process Measures Data Collection Method Is Best?

None of them. Some companies insist that every process be mapped. Others use task analysis. Some prefer a combination, such as process mapping and activity charts. This combination provides the best graphic representation of process flows and the greatest amount of detail about the activities performed. In Chapter 10, "Job and Individual Performance Measures and Management," we describe how to take a comprehensive activity chart and create individual performance profiles.

Endnotes

1. Cokins, Gary. *Activity-Based Cost Management: Making It Work.* Irwin: The McGraw-Hill Companies, 1996.

Job and Individual Performance Measures and Management

10

This chapter is about performance measures at the individual (job) level. However, it's nearly impossible to discuss individual performance measures without discussing performance management. Performance management encompasses planning, doing, appraising, coaching, and compensating work done by an individual. So this chapter will necessarily discuss performance management, as well the methods used to develop individual performance measures. To complicate things even more, there is some debate about who owns performance measurement and performance management. If Human Resources owns the performance system, then companies have the wrong owner. Performance measurement belongs to management because it is a management tool. By extension, performance management, a subset of performance measurement, belongs to management as well.

Problems with Performance Appraisal

In many companies a single performance appraisal form is often used for dozens of jobs with absolutely no link to the strategy or the business plan, or even to the processes. Performance planning and appraisal systems are often annualized, stand-alone processes with few, if any, checkpoints during the year. Further, grade inflation hit the universal form users in the then late 1980s. To remedy the problem many managers turned to some dubious ways to combat grade inflation rather than correct the lack of specificity on the appraisal form. They forced department heads to distribute performance ratings over a group of people that mimicked a normal distribution. On the surface, this seems logical, but it did not improve performance. The distribution method only made employees mad because the distributions were arbitrary. And managers liked it even less because the distribution method caused performance-eroding contention within many departments. Arbitrary distribution defies logic. Who says that performance has to have a normal distribution? Why can't the best company in the world have all excellent-rated employees?!

Rating distributions also made a mockery of competency performance models. The logic behind a competency-based appraisal system is to define a basic set of skills a company needs to be successful. Behind every competency program are many training programs to help employees advance from where they were to where they want or need to be. Theoretically, competencies can be learned. Therefore, every employee can be at the top of the scale, defying the logic of a distribution.

Management By Objective (MBO) was popular for more than 20 years. Unfortunately, MBOs did not work well because they were not tied to a strategic focus, to business plans or to project plans. MBOs were too vague to be useful in measuring daily operations. This led individuals and their managers to weighing business plan objectives more heavily than daily operations with the expected lack of, or wrong kind of, results.

Management's attitude toward performance appraisal is also a factor. Almost all managers hate assessing and rating employee performance. They complain endlessly about the amount of time it takes to complete the appraisal forms and discuss the results. They will spend hours pouring over minutiae in spreadsheets and projects plans for a $100,000 project, but they will scream about spending 10 hours a year appraising $2 million worth of human capital. Coaching people is virtually nonexistent in most companies, despite all the press given to empowering employees. In short, management is always looking for the performance appraisal silver bullet. There isn't one. For all the talk about human and intellectual capital, there is very little evidence that management even wants to be bothered with planning, appraising, and coaching its employees!

If individual performance measures and performance appraisal are so bothersome, why bother at all? Relatively few companies have these measures. But if a company has a variable pay or pay-at-risk plan, good performance measures and a good performance management plan must be in place. The reasons are simple and logical. The purpose of individual performance measures is to link the individual to the organization's strategic focus, the business plan, and to the department's processes. This effort creates greater congruity horizontally and vertically in the organization, increasing organizational alignment. Further, employees want to know the criteria (re: measures) against which their performance will be judged. Finally, the move to pay-for-performance or variable pay systems means even staff workers are demanding reliable and dependable sets of performance measures for each job, each person.

What Is the Origin of Individual Performance Measures?

Individual performance measures come from a variety of sources. Individual performance measures *require* some analysis and planning, but the following set of linkages should provide most managers with a place to start.

Corporate scorecard and strategic focus. If you were to ask employees to describe their company's strategic focus, it's likely that less than 10% could provide the answer. The first task is to link the individual to the strategic focus. Management can do this through the use of common corporate scorecard measures, in the sense that everyone in the company is held accountable for the measures. Many companies have common measures for expense avoidance as part of an overall operationally focused strategy. Management must also spend many hours communicating its strategic focus, not just this year's business objectives. The communication must be frequent and often, not just once a year.

Business Plan. Establishing the link between the business plan and the employee can be straightforward. In many companies the rules are simple: each employee will be responsible for one or more objectives on the business plan. And from the authors' experience, management should not make it any more complicated than that.

Processes: linking the individual to any processes that person might touch. The source of most individual measures will come from processes he or she works on. This only makes sense. Individuals or groups of individuals perform all the activities within a process.

Collecting Process Information

There are three ways to collect process information that can then lead to individual performance measures.

1. Process maps
2. Function charts
3. Task analysis

Process maps

Process maps are excellent data sources for individual performance measures. Once the tasks in a process map are identified, performance measures for customers, quality, quantity, cycle time, and costs can be generated. Exhibit 10.1 represents a 1-800-Telephony Sales Process map of the complete customer ordering process at major activity levels.

The information from the process map can be replicated in a table format (Exhibit 10.2) to help develop performance measures. The major activities are listed in the left column. The second column lists the outcome of that activity. The customer measures, quality, quantity, cycle time, and costs columns have appropriate performance measures for each activity. This information is based on time studies, feedback from customers, and employee input.

Function charts

These provide the most detail for any job. Function charts list all the major activities performed in a process down the left column, much like what was done in Exhibit 10.2. Next, all the people, organizations, or systems with whom or with which the process has contact are listed

Exhibit 10.1 *1-800-Telephony Sales Process*

across the top row. At the intersection of an activity and a contact, the specific activity is noted. The function chart example covers the work done by a benefits and payroll call center associate.

The function chart in Exhibit 10.3 covers only most of the relationships the call center representative has with other people, systems, or organizations. The advantage of the function chart is that it provides a detailed listing of all the activities performed by a call center representative. But the downside is that all that information must be converted into something useful. In many cases this is an excellent time to use competencies to view work being performed. See the dimension section at the end of the chapter for some examples of competencies.

Task analysis

Discussions with call center representatives and their managers helped determine which activities were major. Performance measures from those discussions yielded the following set of activities:

- Cooperation with other call center representatives
- Depth of business knowledge
- Empathizing with customer
- Identifying trends in the customer data
- Increased use of technology

Exhibit 10.2
1-800-Telephony Sales

Task/Activity	Quality	Quantity	Mean Cycle Time	Cost/$*
Take order	100% accuracy	>60 tpd/CSR*	7.5 minutes	1.25
Credit check	100% correct approval	60 tpd/CSR	0.03 minutes	0.49
Pick goods	100% accuracy	>90	4.5 minutes	0.75
Label package	100% accuracy	>280	1.5 minutes	0.25
Delivery		>60 tpd	<48 hours	3.15
Total			13.56	6.38

Exhibit 10.3
Sales Associate Function Chart

Dependencies/Tasks	Customer (Employee)	Sales Screen Order	PeopleSoft Comp	Expert Advisor	Exchange
Benefits Consulting	• Take customer order	• Use to verify address, mail code, and any personal info. • Use to confirm process dates of info (pay, and personal, org, CC) changed on profile (history)	• Use to view paychecks and various deductions • Use to look at history of ee's benefits (date changes and status changes) • Use to view current selection of benefits • Use to view COBRA	• Document calls • Confirm history of calls • Use to transfer items that need to be researched • Use to log in forms and checks	• Use to keep team informed of any communications regarding problems, concerns, issues, and general information
Payroll Consulting	• Provide customer service regarding their pay questions	• Use to confirm process dates of info (pay, and personal, org, CC) changed on profile (history)	• Use to verify salary YTD, • Use to view paychecks and various deductions • Use to determine if group benefits were deducted correctly • Use to view damaged check reprints • Use to verify awards and amounts and what CC used	• Document calls • Confirm history of calls • Use to transfer items that need to be researched	• Use to keep team informed of any communications regarding problems, concerns, issues, and general information
HR Policy/ Procedure Consulting	• Provide customer service regarding their policy and procedure questions	• Use to verify HR data		• Document calls • Confirm history of calls • Use to transfer items that need to be researched	• Use to keep team informed of any communications regarding problems, concerns, issues, and general information
Call Distribution/ Call Directing		• Use to document calls • Use to confirm history of calls • Use to transfer items that need to be researched	• Use to keep team informed of any communications regarding problems, concerns, issues, and general information		
Severance Lump Sum Processing	• Provide customer service regarding ee's lump sum questions	• Use to verify address and any personal info, severance dates and retirement eligibility	• Use to verify if/when lump sum check is issued	• Use to document lump sum form rec'd and severance info	• Use to keep team informed of any communications regarding problems, concerns, issues, and general information

- Keeping agreements with customers
- On-line documentation of customer concerns
- Openness to new ideas
- Organization of work
- Pay sheet entries
- Pre- and post-payday attendance
- Production
- Project communication
- Referencing other sources of information
- Responsiveness to customer concerns
- Teamwork with other call center representatives

These activities (tasks) were then placed in a performance profile. A performance profile is a basic report card for appraising the work of an employee. See this section at the end of the chapter.

Focus Groups

There are other methods of establishing and communicating corporate scorecard measures. The management of a property and casualty insurance company linked all its employees to their corporate scorecard by simply holding focus groups with employees in each job's family. Within the company, there were over 60 named jobs in the compensation database. A performance measurement team held focus groups with position holders in each job (e.g., in actuarial). The actuaries were shown the corporate scorecard, which gave all employees their introduction. Each employee was asked to write all the possible performance measures he or she could think of that related to or supported those in the corporate scorecard. The lists were long, and the participants were asked to vote on which performance measures they had control over and on which they had some relationship to the corporate scorecard. Those measures with the highest vote count were kept as the first round of measures. The facilitators of the focus groups:

- Collected all the suggestions and built a database of performance measures
- Refined all the performance measures from the focus group and shared them with management
- Got management consensus on which measures were to be included
- Made consensus measures part of the job's performance profile

- Provided all project participants feedback from the performance measurement team

The rule of thumb: for every hour spent identifying performance measures, you will spend an additional 10 hours refining them, including getting management approval. This focus group method takes about two and one half hours for each job. But the final results are performance measures linked to the corporate scorecard and agreed to by both management and employees.

Putting It All Together

The best innovations in performance management took place on the periphery of business and psychology. There was not so much a frontal attack on the old methods as there were new ways of analyzing and conducting business. Primarily, innovations in performance measures have come from activity-based costing, activity-based management, and TQM. The common theme that runs through these methods is that controlling variance in human behavior can only be successfully accomplished at the task level. Further, the controlling mechanism (i.e., the performance measures) must focus on the activity *and* the result in order to ensure uniform performance. The activity-based management model of performance management is a process concerned with activities (i.e., goals, objectives, tasks, action steps, competency, or behavior) of the individual. There are two fundamental reasons for this:

1. In all companies, most processes are performed by their employees. Individual behavior is the primary source of all variance in non-machine-controlled activity. From a TQM point of view, managing individual activities is equal to process control. If management wants to control human processes, then management must measure the *activities* performed by individual employees rather than just the results.
2. In most modern companies, the results of what employees do may not be seen for days, months, or even years. It is imperative that management measures the employees' activities, because it is the only control on future results available to them.

The Performance Profile

Performance profile is just another word for a performance appraisal form. But there are some fundamental differences between a typical performance appraisal form and a performance profile. First and foremost, the performance profile covers all the activities being performed by an employee. Second, it covers the outcomes of each activity. Third, it has target performance measures that measure either the activity, the outcome, or both. Fourth, it lists the data sources that will be used to judge an employee's performance. We list here the minimum requirements for a successful performance profile. (See Exhibits 10.4, 10.5, and 10.6.)

Sections. Each performance profile should contain the same perspective as those listed in the corporate scorecard: financial, customer satisfaction, organizational capability, operational excellence, growth and innovation perspectives, and business objective sections. These sections often contain a set of measures from the corporate scorecard to be shared by all employees. This effort links all employees to the business strategy. Descriptions of each section follow.

- *Financial results section.* In this section the manager and his or her immediate supervisor should negotiate the financial outcome of their particular unit. Financial outcomes may include combined ratios, expenses, economic value added, return on assets, return on benefits, etc.
- *Customer satisfaction section.* This section focuses on increasing customer satisfaction with the overall goal of retaining current customers. Some possible activities to be addressed include increasing the measurement of customer encounters; the development of a customer satisfaction index; and tracking products features that customers find valuable.
- *Organizational capability section.* The human resource management section identifies three to five human resource activities, outcome, measures, data sources, and time frames that are critical to the success of the organization. Such activities are increasing team work and cooperation; developing the overall quality of leadership skills; increasing the degree and quality of communication; developing people; and improving performance management.

- *Operational excellence section.* Operational excellence is primarily concerned with the productivity concepts of cost, cycle time, conformance to standards, quantity, and quality. There are often overlaps between operational excellence and other sections, such as customer satisfaction, where solving a customer problem efficiently increases productivity.
- *Growth and innovation section.* Each employee will be held accountable for continuous improvement of the business and himself or herself, and the adoption and diffusion of innovations and improvements. This ensures that each employee understands and is rewarded for continuous improvement and innovation.
- *Business objectives section.* Once the business plan objectives are identified and agreed upon, each person is held accountable for achieving one or more of them. This ties the person to the business plan.

Definition of Performance Profile Terms

The new performance profile has some concepts and terms that may be new to most managers. The template for developing a performance profile is illustrated in Exhibit 10.4.

- **Activities.** "Activities" describes the work an individual is asked to accomplish. "Activities" is an inclusive term from activity-based management which covers goals, objectives, processes, duties, tasks, action steps, and elements. Almost all activities used in profiles are written at the task level. This could also include any links to service level agreements between departments. See Chapter 9, "Process Performance Measures." The following examples are for a sales associate. The activities shown are for the customer satisfaction section of the performance profile. Other sections of the performance profile are developed in the same manner.
- **Outcomes.** Every activity has an outcome or an output, the end result of the activity being performed. Sometimes the outcome is a restatement of the activity or target. But it is vital for everyone to understand what outcome each activity produces, so that both the activities and the outcome have appropriate performance measures. In this example, the outcomes involve the customer. Why do we empathize with the customer? So the customer will think he or she is cared about personally. See Exhibit 10.5.

Exhibit 10.4
Customer Service Representative Performance Profile

Activity	Outcomes	Target Measures	Data Source
Customer Satisfaction			
Empathizing with customer	•	•	•
Keeping agreements	•	•	•
Responsiveness	•	•	•
Depth of business knowledge	•	•	•
Referencing	•	•	•

Exhibit 10.5
Customer Service Representative Performance Profile

Activity	Outcomes	Target Measures	Data Source	Rating
Customer Satisfaction				
Empathizing with customer	• A satisfied customer			
Keeping agreements	• A satisfied customer			
Responsiveness	• A satisfied customer			
Depth of business knowledge	• An educated customer			
Referencing	• An educated customer			

- **Target Measures.** Target measures establish the measurement criteria for either the activity being performed or the outcome, or both. Whenever possible, target measures should be quantitative; but this is not an absolute rule. See Exhibit 10.6.
- **Data Sources.** The data source column identifies the source used to make an appraisal and/or by whom. For example, the data source for teamwork and cooperation could be observation by team members, feedback from managers, 360 degree feedback, or citations from team members. Logs, audits, reports, surveys, counts, etc., are also data sources. See examples in Exhibit 10.7.

Exhibit 10.6
Customer Service Representative Performance Profile

Activity	Outcomes	Target Measures	Data Source	Rating
Customer Satisfaction				
Empathizing with customer	• A satisfied customer	• % use of empathizing language • Support of company policies and products		
Keeping agreements	• A satisfied customer	• % agreements kept or follow thru completed		
Responsiveness	• A satisfied customer	• % satisfied customers • All potential questions probed and answered		
Depth of business knowledge	• An educated customer	• Accuracy of consulting • No returned calls		
Referencing	• An educated customer	• No repeat calls from single employee • Increased use of online tools		

Exhibit 10.7
Customer Service Representative Performance Profile

Activity	Outcomes	Target Measures	Data Source	Rating
Customer Satisfaction				
Empathizing with customer	• A satisfied customer	• % use of empathizing language • Support of company policies and products	• Observation • Call/Operation coaching checklist	
Keeping agreements	• A satisfied customer	• % agreements kept or follow thru completed	• Expert Advisor • Call/Operation coaching checklist	
Responsiveness	• A satisfied customer	• % satisfied customers • All potential questions probed and answered	• Expert Advisor • Call/Operation coaching checklist	
Depth of business knowledge	• An educated customer	• Accuracy of consulting • No returned calls	• Call/Operation coaching checklist	
Referencing	• An educated customer	• No repeat calls from single employee	• Customer Satisfaction Index	

- **Ratings.** The ratings column judges, by the use of a scale, the degree to which an individual met, exceeded, or missed the target measure. For example, if a manager exceeds the established target, that manager will be eligible for a T1, S, or E rating, depending on the negotiated and agreed-upon percentages above or below the target. The target rating scheme meets with less grade inflation and better acceptance by employees and managers alike. The complete scale is shown, along with recommended guidelines for establishing the ratings. See Exhibits 10.8 and 10.9.

Exhibit 10.8
Customer Service Representative Performance Profile

Activity	Outcomes	Target Measures	Data Source	Rating
Customer Satisfaction				
Empathizing with customer	• A satisfied customer	• % use of empathizing language • Support of company policies and products	• Observation • Call/Operation coaching checklist	**Th**
Keeping agreements	• A satisfied customer	• % agreements kept or follow thru completed	• Expert Advisor • Call/Operation coaching checklist	**T**
Responsiveness	• A satisfied customer	• % satisfied customers • All potential questions probed and answered	• Expert Advisor • Call/Operation coaching checklist	**T+**
Depth of business knowledge	• An educated customer	• Accuracy of consulting • No returned calls	• Call/Operation coaching checklist	**S**
Referencing	• An educated customer	• No repeat calls from single employee • Increased use of online tools	• Customer Satisfaction Index • Observation	**T**

Exhibit 10.9
Target Rating and Conversion

Target Scale	Qualitative Measures	Quantitative Measures
Threshold (Th)	Below Expectations	80–85%
Target (T) –		86–95%
Target	Meets Expectations	96–105%
Target +		106–115%
Superior (S) –	Exceeds Expectations	116–125%
Superior		126–135%
Superior +	Significantly Exceeds Expectations	136–145%

The Performance Management Cycle

Performance management is a cyclical process. It starts with planning and ends in the compensation of the individual for the previous year's performance.

Planning	Developing either the business objectives or the performance measures for which an individual or a team will be held accountable for the upcoming performance year
Doing	Performing the activities necessary to reach a desired outcome
Appraising	Appraising, evaluating, or judging how well an individual or team achieves expected results (goals)
Coaching	Developing relationships with others in order to influence them to achieve the agreed-upon performance (i.e., objectives) through: constructive feedback via conversations which focus on the behavior, process, and/or result(s) vs. personality; and, modeling of desired behaviors
Compensation	Rewarding or sanctioning employees based on the way they performed the activities, the quality or quantity of the outcomes, and the degree to which they met their target measures. See Exhibit 10.10.

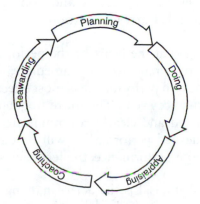

Exhibit 10.10 Performance Management Cycle

Details of Performance Management

If we are to achieve high performance as both individuals and team members/leaders, it's important for every one of us to have a clear understanding of our role in and our contribution to our organization's mission. Having clearly stated activities, outcomes, target measures and data sources leads to a better understanding of our value to the business. Clearly written business plan objectives are critical to success. So, too, are the activities performed on a daily basis.

When developing and/or reviewing the performance profile, keep the following questions in mind:

- What *specific* outcome am I trying to achieve?
- What is the specific product or service of this objective? For whom?
- By *when*? Is this result achievable within the plan year or sooner? If not, what products, services or result can be expected within the plan year to help me achieve the longer-term objectives?
- What is my direct (expected) contribution to my organization's financial results? If I am in a staff area, how do I directly support financial goals of the businesses I serve (i.e., value-added, cost benefit)?
- What are the expectations/standards of my customers for my products and services?

Agreeing on performance measures. For performance management to work effectively, it is critical that everyone agree to *what* specifically will be measured and *how* it will be measured. Be sure that what constitutes threshold performance levels and above-target performance levels is determined and clearly understood.

Coaching. Coaching is at the heart of the performance management process. Effective coaching must be immediate, frequent, and non-judgmental. Feedback on performance is most effective when it follows soon after a performance event. The more frequent the feedback and the more substantiated and clearly communicated the feedback, the more quickly the desired performance will be developed and maintained. In cases of poor performance, the feedback should be impartial.

Formal appraisal. Appraisal is the act of judging an employee's performance against some criteria. In the performance profile, the criteria are the target measures. Because the performance profile is a performance profile, less completion time is required, which means that more time can be spent on the interactive conversation about this performance period's results.

Guidelines for Constructive Appraisal of Performance

- Respect the other person's need for privacy. This is particularly true where the appraisal indicates a need for a change/improvement in behavior.
- Make the process interactive: if you are the appraiser allow the employee to offer his/her opinions; or, solicit feedback from the other people that have worked with the employee.
- Focus on the behavior or the activity, not the person.
- Attempt a balance between positive and negative comments.
- Provide useful feedback: alternatives, options, ideas for adjusting performance problems or further enhancing performance.
- Feedback should *only* be offered on observed behavior, not on perceived attitudes. The process itself should be descriptive and objective rather than judgmental and subjective. It should focus on behavior that can be improved/enhanced.
- Behavior, as well as any behavioral change that is required, should be described in objective and concrete terms with specific examples of corrective actions offered whenever/wherever possible. Focusing on the behavior *versus* the person can help to diffuse a spirit of defensiveness.
- An emotional response may only lead to anger and frustration; therefore, feedback should be offered calmly and quietly. Feedback should be extended in an atmosphere of openness and trust and should be solicited through questions rather than pronouncements or statements.
- Constructive criticism should be balanced with a discussion of areas of improvement. As with any process, moderation should be the guide in demonstrating an appreciation for how the recipient of the feedback will interpret and value the feedback.
- Addressing the results of desirable (altered) behavior will help to emphasize the positive and encourage others to work toward that behavior.

- Asking the recipient of the feedback to restate the feedback "communication" will ensure greater understanding and commitment. It will also clarify any areas which require further explanation.
- Feedback should not be viewed as a top-down process from management/team leader to subordinate/team member, but rather as an enabling, interactive, iterative process which includes everyone in the performance management process.

Conclusion

What do General Electric, Hewlett-Packard, Motorola, and Coca-Cola all have in common? They are considered by many to be very successful and by some to be world-class companies. Success in business generally does not occur by chance. It requires strong leadership that executes good management practices. In this book we thoroughly discussed the underlying themes that optimize the competitive position of most companies:

1. Success starts with a focused strategy. There are three different strategic focuses: cost, service, and product focus. Too often, companies don't clearly articulate their strategic direction. If the senior executives can't agree on where the company is going, how can employees focus their efforts on the most strategic areas? Managers who follow the "all-things-to-all-people" approach seldom achieve preeminence in their markets. Why? Despite the hyperbole of "management-by-magazine" rhetoric, it is impossible for management to drive world-class excellence through all facets of their value chain. No company can excel at research and development, marketing, sales, operations, logistics, support functions, and customer service and remain a cost competitor. Success requires strategic focus. Once the strategic focus has been determined, it can be further refined through the creation of a business strategy that is clearly articulated throughout the company.

2. A corporate scorecard is critical because it provides both leading and lagging measures that can be used to assess actual versus planned organizational performance relative to the business strategy. A well-designed scorecard will balance hard and soft measures, focus on the drivers most critical to achieving the business strategy, and link to appropriate business systems (compensation, employee development, etc.).

3. The business plan is the key to closing the gaps between the corporate scorecard results and target measurement. The best business plans are those that define the activities needed to close the gaps, the outcomes of those activities, target measures for both, and what information will evaluate the success or failure of those assigned specific activities.

4. Process measure must support the strategic focus, the containment of cost, reduction of cycle time, and conformance to customer standards.

5. Individual and job performance measures are needed to forge the links among the corporate scorecard, the business plan, and process measures for the employee.

6. Measurement links the employee to the strategy, the corporate scorecard, the business plan, and process measures. But aligning the technology, organizational and process architectures to support the strategic focus enhances additional success.

These six steps are extremely challenging for most companies. They require good "sensing capabilities" to be able to identify gaps between the strategic focus, the business plan, process measures, and the architectures. A conceptual framework, with clearly defined steps to visualize the complex linkage, makes the undertaking somewhat more approachable. We sincerely hope this book provides you with a conceptual framework and the tools and techniques needed to be able to incorporate them into your company.

Index

Process objectives, 71
Process set up time, 7
Product-focused strategy, 4

Q

Qualitative measures, 100
Qualitative measures, manager
    resistance, 100
Quality, 23, 129–134
Quantitative measures, 100
Quantity, 23, 129–134

R

Ratings, distributions, 150
Ratings, performance, 125
Relationship map, 86
Rosenthal, J. Wade, 33

S

Service level agreements,
    135–135
Situation analysis, 36
Southwest Airlines, 19
Standard operating
    procedures, 136
Strassman, Paul, 81
Strategic discipline, 19
Strategic focus, 17
Strategic objectives, 70
Strategic partner, 58
Strategic planning, 34
Strategy, 34
Switching strategies, 28

T

Tableau d'bord, 94
Target measures, 124, 160
Task analysis, 8, 147–148,
    153, 163
Technology architecture, 29, 65
Telephony, 65
Texas Instruments, 8
TQM, 127, 156
Trailing performance
    measures, 6
Treacy, Michael, 18, 33

V

Value chain, 83
Vision, 44, 45

W

Wal-Mart, 2, 4, 20
Weirsama, Fred, 18, 33
Welch, Jack, 6, 31
Work flow, 88
Work plan, 76
World-class customer service, 18

Z

Zachmann, John, 81